The Courage to Care

Pearls from Tears

Robert & Arvella Schuller

Harvest House Publishers
Irvine, California 92714

Scriptures marked NASB are from the NEW AMERICAN STANDARD BIBLE, copy-right © The Lockman Foundation 1960, 1962, 1963, 1968, 1971, 1972, 1973, 1975 and are used by permission.

Scriptures marked RSV are from the REVISED STANDARD VERSION of the Bible, copyright © 1946, 1952, 1971, 1973 and are used by permission.

All other scriptures are from THE LIVING BIBLE, copyright © 1971, Tyndale House Publishers, Wheaton, Illinois. Used by permission.

THE COURAGE OF CAROL

Copyright © 1978 Robert H. Schuller
Published by Harvest House
Irvine, California 92714
Library of Congress Catalog Card Number: 78-65619
ISBN 0-89081-182-2

Printed in the United States of America.

The Courage of Carol

Publisher's Foreword

On Saturday, July 7, 1978, while Dr. and Mrs. Robert Schuller were in Seoul, Korea, completing a three week ministry to chaplains and ministers in the Orient. Word was received that their thirteen-year-old daughter, Carol Lynn Schuller, was gravely injured in a motorcycle accident in Iowa, where she was vacationing with her cousins. "Her left leg has been amputated. Further amputation may be necessary. We cannot say her life is out of danger. She is still in surgery."

With that limited information the Schullers moved into the troubled and untravelled paths of human grief which would see their family's possibility thinking faith tested as never before.

Is possibility thinking a polyanna philosophy as some critics have claimed? Or does it hold the seed to resurrection power in life's cross-bearing experiences?

Through these pages the Schullers open their hearts to you, reserving no secrets to themselves. They have allowed the publisher to include some of the intimate pages from their private diary, which they kept carefully as they walked with God through this storm. This book is their testimony. They want the world to know that the right kind of faith turns tears into pearls of priceless spiritual value.

Table of Contents

1

Shopping
For Pearls

ARVELLA'S DIARY
June 20, 1978

I stretched in my seat—the short nap I had was refreshing. It was a long flight from Los Angeles to Hong Kong and I had started the trip as a tired Mom. The plane was beginning its descent now and we had already broken through the clouds. Far below was the Pacific Ocean with tiny white dots. Were they fishing vessels? Or pearl-diving boats?

I turned the ring on my right hand around and around. It was a favorite one. My husband had given it to me for Christmas many years ago when he returned from the Orient, following a speaking mission for the U.S. Air Force. I fingered the cluster of five pearls . . . "One for each of the children you have given me." Simple, inexpensive, but a treasured symbol of our family love.

Five pearls . . . five children. Just a few hours ago we said good-bye to each other—with the exception of our son, Robert Anthony, who left twenty-four hours before to lead a tour of Bible students to the Holy Land.

It was still dark this morning as we packed our suitcases into the trunk of the car and the six of us crowded into the car for the one hour trip to the L.A. Airport. The first stop was for the 6:30 a.m. flight on Western Airlines. Thirteen-year-old Carol and eleven-year-old Gretchen were going to be visiting their cousins for two and a half weeks on the farm. How they loved the Schuller farm in Iowa where their Daddy was born and grew up. They enjoyed fishing in the same river he fished in as a boy. They would sleep in the house he had helped to build after the tornado had wiped out the entire farm. All the stories Daddy could tell about the farm came alive with each visit.

They talked so excitedly about their cousins—eighteen in all! Would they be much taller and look older? Carol had surely shot up since she last saw them. I noticed that her shoulders were even with mine as we walked to the plane.

"There are no reserved seats, so you may seat them yourself," the stewardess said. Gretchen sat next to the window, clutching her favorite stuffed bear. Carol, feeling too grown up to carry a stuffed animal, left her brown and white dog, a gift from her daddy, lying on her bed pillow in her room. Now as we said good-bye, Gretchen's lip suddenly quivered and her face puckered up, "I'm going to miss you, Mom." But Carol, assuming the grown-up sister role, quickly affirmed, "We are going to have a wonderful time. Don't you worry, Mom!" And with a quick kiss I left.

Another child, another pearl. At 7:35 a.m.—only one hour later—we, the remaining Schullers, said our good-byes to Jeannie our twenty-year-old college sophomore. She was going to study in Israel for the summer and had to report to the campus at Wheaton, Illinois, for two weeks of preparatory study before the trip to the Middle

East. We would not see her again until Thanksgiving.

Sheila, our remaining pearl, and our oldest daughter, finally ushered us to our flight to Hong Kong. She was excited about remaining at home, for she was very much in love. "Sheila," her daddy ordered, "if you should become engaged while we are gone, I want you to telephone us, no matter where we are. Your mom and I want to be the first to know." With that happy order, we said good-bye.

Five pearls—five children now scattered from us; yet we were all held together by that invisible string of love which was rooted in a positive Christian faith—a string of pearls. I turned to Bob seated next to me and interrupted his reading, "Honey, we are going to be in some good shopping centers—Singapore, Hong Kong, Seoul, Korea. I think I will shop for a string of pearls to match my ring."

"*Hmm*, okay, that's a great idea," Bob answered. Then he added, "Did you know that the pearl is a natural symbol of possibility thinking? An unwelcome, irritating grain of sand invades the comforting privacy of an oyster's sheltered and easy existence to inflict relentless pain. Immediately, instinctively, the hurting oyster deposits around the torturing grain of sand, a rich and rare liquid—a form of tears. These precious tears will harden to form a glistening globe sheltering the tender oyster from the uninvited agony. So the soft little creature naturally reacts positively to the accident and turns its tear into a pearl."

2
A Bad News Phone Call

⏤◍⏤

BOB'S DIARY
Saturday, July 8 (Korea)
Friday, July 7 (U.S.A.)

I'm resting now for the first time since I started this demanding trip to minister to enthusiastic Korean Christians. Arvella has gone with the church women to Prayer Mountain. Perhaps I'll have my first chance to go shopping and hopefully find a simple string of pearls and surprise her.

This week I have lectured two hours every morning and two hours every night to an audience each time of over 10,000 ministers. They can—and I believe *will* change the future of the Orient! "Who can count all the apples in one seed!"

I had reserved today for rest, for tomorrow I would be speaking at three Sunday church services. And then we will catch a plane tomorrow evening to go home to America. But right now I am just praising God for His goodness!

I reflect on my family. Arvella is having—as I am—a great walk with our Living Lord Jesus Christ, who really lives in these Christians we've met here. Right now, Bob Jr. is in the Holy Land. Sheila is at home! How happy she sounded when she telephoned us in Hong Kong a week ago to tell us Jim Coleman had proposed marriage. "You should see my diamond, Dad! How does a February wedding sound?" Nothing is greater than a long distance telephone call that brings good news! Jeanne is in college in Wheaton, Illinois; Carol and Gretchen are enjoying their uncles, aunts and cousins in Iowa.

As I rested, I glanced at the clock. It was 3:45. Suddenly my thoughts were interrupted by the ringing of the telephone. I picked it up and heard the voice of Mike Nason, my television producer calling from America. I'm lying in bed as we exchange our usual opening greetings. My heart is calm for I've never had a "bad news phone call" while overseas. Then Mike said, "Bob, Carol has been in an accident—motorcycle. They may have to amputate her left leg. She's in the emergency room now in Sioux City, Iowa. (My heart skipped—having grown up in that area I knew that really serious cases were always rushed the fifty miles to Sioux City.) Mike went on: "Here's the hospital number if you want to call. Your brother, Henry, is at the hospital. Sheila is preparing to fly out, and should be there soon."

"Thanks Mike." I tried to swallow the lump in my throat. "I will try to get a plane out tonight. Oh, but Northwest Airlines is on strike, and I'm told there's a six week waiting list. But, Mike assume that we will get on the K.A.L. flight that leaves here in five hours. Arrange the fastest connections from our arrival in L.A. to Sioux City. And incidentally, Mike, I'm glad *you* gave me the news. It makes it easier to take." I knew Mike understood what I was feeling for I have watched him father his beautiful brain-damaged Tara—who is unable to walk!

"Oh, one thing more, Bob," Mike added, "the word I get is that Carol's attitude and spirit is fantastic!" Somehow, that last line was God's hint that my tears could be turned into a costly but precious string of spiritual pearls.

I put the phone down. I found myself pacing the room— alone. I was shaking now. When would Arvella be back? I telephoned the room of my travelling companion and associate, Wilbert Eichenberger, hoping he'd be there. He answered. "Ike, this is Bob, can you come to my room a minute?" "Sure, Bob." Within minutes he was there sharing the shock and offering to try to arrange the details for our early exit.

3
The First Tears
of a Pearl

ARVELLA'S DIARY
Saturday, July 8, (Korea)
Friday, July 7, (U.S.A.)

My knuckle rapped three times on the door to Room #1500. Instantly, it flew open and Bob held me for a moment. I saw that Ike was in the room and on the telephone and I immediately began to relate what a wonderful day it had been—only to be stopped short by Bob. "We have bad news, but it could be worse. Carol has been in an accident and has a badly mangled leg. She is in Sioux City and I've talked to the doctor. One artery is severed and he is doubtful that they can save the leg."

Calmly, very calmly, I walked to the window and looked out. Carol? Our Carol? Our softball player, horse rider, snow skier, water skier—so excited about being thirteen, her first year as a teenager and so full of life, so boundless with energy?

Carol, alone without her dad or mom . . . Carol, how much pain . . .? Carol, you must keep your leg. It is possible! Just yesterday morning I heard again the importance of visualizing in prayer time. Bob had shared with 10,000 people through an interpreter how to visualize healing in prayer. Now I must visualize for Carol's sake: Her leg being slowly repaired, the severed artery somehow being attached. There is no hysteria, no tears, only a tremendous calm . . . .

With an intense concentration of all my thoughts, I was prayerfully visualizing the mangled leg being repaired, right now in surgery, and at the same time, praying, "Oh Jesus Christ, surround Carol with Your loving presence and give her the strength to cope with the pain."

Methodically and numbly, I reached for the suitcases. We must get packed and catch the first plane home. I hear Bob say, "Ike is trying to get us on the 9:00 flight tonight. It is the only flight until tomorrow night." I nod as he continues, "I'm going to call Dr. Cho now and see if he will excuse me from Sunday's speaking commitments. I've already asked Ike to fill the speaking engagement tonight. I'll be back as soon as I can."

Alone, I walk again to the window and find myself repeating the same prayer—only to be interrupted by the ring of the telephone.

It's Sheila calling from the U.S.A. "Mom, Carol is in surgery now, and they are amputating her leg." I sit on the bed, hold my head in my hands and gasp, "Oh, no, not her leg." And then the tears begin to fall. Sheila continued, "I'm ready to leave now, and I'll be there soon."

Somehow I manage to say, "Sheila, have someone telephone Jeanne. I don't know if we can get on tonight's plane. It may take awhile to get there. I'm so glad you are going to Carol. You will be a great comfort to her." I put the phone down and weep, but only for a few minutes.

Calm once more, I return to the most important job, to pack carefully, leaving out a change of clothes for in-flight. And then I wait . . . .

Bob returned and with my voice breaking, I told him Carol was losing her leg. Again we held each other. Finally recovering, Bob reminded me, "There is a dinner party at 5:30 and we should try to attend. We should try to eat something some time this evening. At least we can make an appearance."

At the dinner party everyone was gracious as the news spread fast. Somehow, the conversation moved from one topic to another. There were times when the tears almost surfaced but I would turn and ask a question of someone to try to keep my thoughts from Carol. I try to comment about the delicous food—and it is, only it doesn't go down very easily.

The dessert is brought out, and Mr. Cha proudly presents my husband with a chocolate soufflé. We are interrupted by a message saying there is no space on tonight's flight. Immediately, Mr. Cha asks us to excuse him and his lovely wife. They tell us they will go to the airport, and we are to leave for the airport at 7:00 p.m. and believe that he will get us on. He speaks with such authority and confidence that I believe him at once, even though we have already heard two times this evening that all seats had been booked six weeks in advance.

Pastor and Mrs. Cho beautifully and gently support us as we check out of the hotel and drive to the airport. There at the curbside is Mr. Cha with his hand waving in the air holding two red boarding passes. Not only did he succeed in getting us on, he also arranged for our baggage to be checked through customs and security without Bob and I waiting in the long lines or sitting in the crowded airport lobby. We were ushered into a quiet room and there the six of us waited and prayed.

Pastor Cho quoted Romans 8:28: "All things work together for good . . ."

GOD WILL BRING GREAT GOOD FROM THIS!

Then Mrs. Cha, in Korean, urgently said "We must pray." And so we reached for each other's hands as she began to pray in Korean. Mrs. Cho, the pastor's wife, then prayed in Korean. Around the circle we prayed.

Strengthened by this mighty circle of powerful prayer partners, I hear the words come from me,

"Dear God—How I thank you that you love Carol more than we do!
Guide the hands of the surgeons now.
Jesus, You are the healing Physician.
Surround Carol now with Your holy and healing presence . . . ."

A tremendous bond of love and power came together in that airport, and tears flowed that were tied together with a cord of love. We didn't know it then but this was to be God's string of pearls.

4
Alleluia! Alleluia!

❧◦◦◦❧

BOB'S DIARY
Korean Air Lines,
Flight #2 Seoul to Los
Los Angeles 9:40 p.m.,
Saturday, July 9 (Korea)

The plane is jammed! But we are going to be on it! A miracle! How did Cha arrange it? Only minutes ago we were still praying—six of us—in a special VIP lounge. "All things work together for good," Pastor Cho was saying, "We cannot understand it now, but God will work this out for many blessings!"

I had quoted that same verse and offered identical counsel to families in my twenty-eight years as a pastor. But now for the first time, I found them unconvincing. I didn't doubt them; but I couldn't imagine how the promise could be fulfilled in the future.

I heard my own sermons coming back to me, "It's not what happens to you, but how you react to what happens to you that matters." "Trouble never leaves you where it finds you—choose by an act of will to accept positively what you cannot change and you will find strength and peace flowing to you according to your need."

"Time to go, Dr. Schuller." Dr. Cho was speaking. It was a short, brisk walk through corridors where special security forces waved us through without us showing our passports. Our Korean friends took us to the ramp of the plane. Wet eyed, we shook hands—and now we are seated in the spacious seats up front. The engines roar as we leave the ground and suddenly we are airborne. "Carol," I call out to her silently in my sould, "hang on—Dad and Mom are on the way home." It will take us ten hours to get to Honolulu; two hours to go through customs there; then another five hours to L.A. I had no idea what connections we'd have from L.A. to Sioux City.

It's ten o'clock at night. I see the stewardess and notice—both legs, two feet. Carol only has one now! It gets to me. I have dropped tears but have not broken down to sob with groaning sounds. I can hold it back no longer. I go to the lavatory and the loud-sounding grief pours out of my mouth, the way an uncontrolled seasick person vomits! Immediately, I am mentally "re-hearing" the 10,000 plus Korean pastors praying out loud in their prayer time "Alleluia—Praise the Lord."

An incredible, unreal "possibility idea" filters into my mind as I internally unload my grief: "Schuller, if you have to bawl, turn it into a ball! Praise God while you cry." And then I hear myself shaping the loud mournful sounds that are pouring from my mouth, shaping them into vowels: "Al-le-lu-ia." Again, "Al-le-lu-ia." And gradually, mysteriously, the sobbing is quietly replaced with sweet serenity! Tears have already turned to pearls through praise!

I dry my tears, regain composure, and plan to return to

my seat. Still in prayer, I ask God, "Lord, how can I really handle this loss? It's okay to bawl like I did, but it better not happen too often."

I walked back to my seat. Again, I notice a young lady across the aisle. Her legs are crossed. I notice her slender left ankle and again I feel the grief returning, threatening me to lose control again. "God, help me," I pleaded silently with open eyes. Into my mind came this message—"It's only a leg. She only lost a leg. You're exaggerating it way out of proportion! She hasn't really lost anything too important! She wants to be a veterinarian, she still can be. She loves to play the violin, guitar, and piano. She still can. She has only lost a leg!"

Then came a sentence that seemed to incapsulate God's special message. It was as if the Holy Spirit entered my soul in my praise through tears in the lavatory and was now shaping pearls of comfort and truth in this sentence, *"Play it down and pray it up!* Play it down! Yes— she only lost a leg. Pray it up! Yes—God can turn her scar into her star, too!

I am convinced that sentence came from the Spirit, for it would comfort and inspire me day-after-day-after-day. Suddenly, the darkness through the black porthole seemed to hold the unseen presence of My Best Friend!

5
Three Dawns in One Day

❧◎Ⅲ◎☙

ARVELLA'S DIARY
Over the Pacific

The night seems dark and long. In reality, it is a short night, for we are traveling east and only six hours from now the dawn will break. There is little or no talking; just a tremendous feeling of "being one"—Bob and I as we go through our first tragedy together.

There is no sleep. I close my eyes but over-and-over again, all I can see is Carol lying in the dark in a ditch in terrible pain. If only I could have been with her . . . There are no thoughts of guilt, and I am surprised. Often I had feelings of guilt as I left the children for a trip with my husband. Whether it was for work or rest, if I knew the children were in good hands, I would decide to be with my husband. How often I thought—and the thought would be a prayer—"Jesus, keep them safe." Now it has happened. . . . I am on a trip and there is an accident. How I want to be there. "Oh, Carol, how did you stand the pain?"

The tears flowed fast and often and the Kleenex piled up. The stewardess quietly and gently would gather them as she walked up and down the aisle.

Bob left his seat and I looked out of the window toward the Eastern sky where a blue light began to outline the thick layer of clouds beneath us.

It was light enough now to read without awakening the passengers around us, so I reached for the Bible I had packed into my flight bag and opened it to the Living Psalms. My eyes searched for comfort and fell to the last portion of Psalm 57, verse 7: *"O God, my heart is quiet and confident"* Yes, there was not the faintest twinge of guilt. And Bob and I *were confident* that Carol was in God's hands.

I read on. *"No wonder I can sing your praises! Rouse yourself, my soul! Arise, O harp and lyre! Let us greet the dawn with song!"* Amazing! I looked out to see that right now the dawn was coloring the dark sky with a deep rich royal blue.

"I will sing your praises among the nations." I thought of the many pastors and church leaders who listened so intently as Bob shared the possibilities of a positive Christian faith: *"When faced with a mountain, I will not quit . . . ."* I remembered how a young Chinese man stood up and shared how Bob's book, *Self-Love*, saved him from suicide, and how he is now experiencing an exciting ministry in the name of Jesus Christ. I thought of the young Indonesian pastor and wife who have such a vibrant faith. They were so poor physically and so lonely for Christian support in a Hindu society. And I remembered how they were inspired and how their tears turned to joy as we promised we would help them.

We had been singing praises among the nations— Hong Kong, Singapore, Bali, then Korea where the response was overwhelming. We, who had come to inspire and uplift others, were ourselves the recipients of tremendous power through prayer and praise; through the "Alleluia," "God is so Good," and "Amen" responses from people who sat in overflow lobbies on mats. Such love, and such power flowed to us as we spoke and shared what was an unforgettable experience.

Yes, we had been singing God's praises among the nations.

"Your kindness and love are as vast as the heavens." I looked out of the window and there was no ending to the scenic panorama of layered clouds now pink and purple with the dawn about to rise. Yes, God's *kindness and love* was all around me.

"Your faithfulness is higher than the skies." How high were we now? 35,000? 40,000 feet? I looked up and the sky had no ending, and I became overwhelmed with the presence of the Almighty God whose *kindness, goodness* and *love* I had just begun to tap.

"I will thank You publicly throughout the Land." I feel deep within that this tragedy will be turned by God into a triumph—our tears into pearls. And we always praise God for His goodness.

We had crossed the International Date Line and gained the day we had lost on our way to the Orient. As we landed in Hawaii to go through customs, it was now Saturday noon and I quickly telephoned the hospital in Sioux City. "Please connect me with anyone who is with Carol Schuller," I said to the receptionist at the hospital switchboard. A voice came over the wire—it was Jeanne. "Jeanne, I'm so glad you are there. How is Carol?" "Her vital signs are stable," Jeanne assured me, adding, *"Her spirit is great.* Sheila is here with me, too."

As I hung up the phone, I heard the words announcing, "Flight #64 to Los Angeles—now boarding." This was a flight I did not want to miss. Reassured, I ran to join

Bob on to Honolulu to the L.A. lap of the trip.

It was night again when we reached Los Angeles, where Mike Nason greeted us. "Athalea Clark has leased a Lear jet and it's waiting for you. Let's go." One hour later our Leat jet reached the altitude of 50,000 feet and we were again high enough to see the dawning over the Rocky Mountains. For a second time we saw the rising dawn, more brilliant than the dawning we saw three hours before above the Pacific. And my heart rejoiced as together Bob and I repeated our Psalm, *"Let us greet the dawn with a song! For God's love and kindness are as vast as the heavens. His faithfulness is as high as the skies."*

Now the silver jet started its descent. As it lost altitude we lost sight of the dawn and landed in darkness. It was 4:04 a.m. in Sioux City, Iowa, and we were back into darkness once more. It was at Carol's bedside that we saw the dawn for the third time. Never before in our lives did we experience three dawns in one day. God would not let us forget. He was saying "Trust me! Believe me! I can turn your tears into pearls!"

6
Every Friend
a Pearl

"Every friend is a pearl." I thank God for Athalea Clark for making this private plane available. "Yes, every true friend is a pearl of great price," I thought as our slender, bullet-shaped jet approached the deserted Sioux City airport.

"Look, Bob" Arvella remarked. She pointed to the landing lights stretched toward us. Not far from one end a string of intersecting lights formed a perfect lighted cross on the otherwise black field. It looked for all the world as if our Tower of Hope, with the lighted cross, was lying on the Iowa field. The runway lights were the lighted cross—the long, brightly lit landing strip was the Tower. I remembered in building our tower my conviction that the lights should always be on. Here there would be a light that never goes out; an ear that is never shut; a heart that never grows cold; and eye that never closes.

We stepped down the small steps dropping to the ground, and walked briskly through a deserted lobby to the street, where a car had just pulled up. Sheila jumped out—her long blonde hair blowing in the wind was lighted in the night by the lobby entrance. Her arms were outstretched as she ran to us. We both noticed her face was aglow with the brightest, most joyful radiance I had ever seen. "Oh, Dad," she called out before she could reach us. "Oh, Mom, you'll be so proud of your daughter." This was no act; no false pretense to give us strength. She was obviously on a spiritual high—higher than I'd ever seen her. "You can't imagine, Dad, how tremendously strong and brave and positive your thirteen-year-old Carol is! You'll be so proud of her!"

We loaded our luggage into the car and drove through the dying night to the hospital fifteen minutes away.

As we parked the car in the almost empty parking lot I noticed the dawn was about to break for the third time for us that day! I could really greet this day with a song! It was Sunday morning! Was this the day God had made? Would we—could we—rejoice and be glad in it?

Strongly, surely, I rejoice! I feel strong and good inside and outside. I can only declare and believe this was the result of our being surrounded by the presence of God! Of course! The church services were just being completed in Korea—the services I was supposed to have led! 12,000 strong, they had focused all their prayers on us. How God was fulfilling His promise!

"Fear not for when you go through the fire it will not consume you. For I am your God. I have redeemed you. I know your name. I will be with you."

In a moment now we would see our darling Carol. Could I handle that? Would I be strong then?

7

Together in Intensive Care

❦◈❧

ARVELLA'S DIARY
At Carol's Bedside
4:30 a.m.—Sunday
July 9

As the car quietly and quickly made its way through deserted streets toward the hospital, I thought again about a coversation Bob and I had had somewhere in flight. How will we know . . .

   . . . when to be sympathetic?
   . . . when to be stern?
   . . . when to be gentle?
   . . . when to discipline?
   . . . when to be tough?
   . . . when to be tender?

What will we say to her? Who will speak first? "Lord," I prayed, "I don't want to cry when I see her. Help me to be strong. How we need Your wisdom and Your guidance to really help Carol through this tough time."

Sheila led the way down the hospital corridor, through the double doors marked "Intensive Care Unit" and then, there we were in Carol's dimly lit room. Seated beside Carol keeping watch was Jeanne, who had been the first to arrive at her bedside.

The expression of joy on Carol's face was the first thing I noticed. Her hoarse and weak voice greeted us through her oxygen mask and there were no tears!

"Hi, Mom! Hi, Dad!" For a moment her voice seemed to choke, but her smile became victorious. Instantly, I saw the same Carol that would walk up to bat determined *not* to strike out, but to get a base hit and maybe even a home run for her team—and I knew she would be all right.

Then I noticed the large, white bandaged short limb hanging in mid-air. The toes of her other foot, with their beautifully manicured nails, touched the bottom of her bed. Tubes seemed to be coming from all parts of her body, and above her head the heart monitor displayed a regular pattern. But everywhere I looked there were black and blue bruises and abrasions. Her body and face were so swollen.

How I wanted to embrace her, but immediately drew back for as I touched her bed there was a cry of pain. I had to be content to stroke the foot and toes of her one leg, then slowly, ever so gently I touched her cheeks and her forehead. She seemed like a wounded bird imprisoned in a white cage.

"I think I know why this accident happened, Dad," she said as she looked at him with piercing eyes. I expected her to give some details and technical answers about how the accident happened, but we would have to learn those by bits and pieces later. Instead, she now spoke in spiritual tones: "God was testing me. God has a special ministry for me to people who have been hurt like

I am hurt." Here was our daughter already ministering to us. Her voice was calm—no hysteria—so grown up. Her mind was as clear as a night sky above the desert.

Yes, God was already turning our tears into pearls. As I motioned to Jeanne and my sister to come with me from the room, leaving Carol with her dad, I heard her say, "I now have four pastors, Dad. There is Pastor Voogd, who I was helping this week. He came to see me as soon as he heard. There is Pastor Van, Grandma's pastor, and there is the hospital Chaplain whom I met today. And then of course there is you!"

The sedative given by the nurse was taking effect now and Carol, feeling secure with her father's hand on hers, drifted into blessed sleep.

8
Rich Pearls
of Faith

❦

BOB'S DIARY
Sunday Morning
July 9

I was struck with the realization that the times we shared with our children Bible stories, Bible memorization, Sunday school, church, and a positive faith, were only the beginnings of what were to become rich pearls of faith.

"As I was lying in the ditch," Carol shared with me, "I kept remembering the words, 'When I walk through the valley of the shadow of death, I will not fear for Thou art with me.' It was so dark and lonely in that ditch, Daddy. I felt like I was going to die. But I kept repeating that verse over and over again."

In that black time as the blood flowed from her mangled leg, Carol didn't realize how near death she had come. We found out later that she lost seventeen pints of blood! "Most was lost in the ditch, the rest was lost in surgery," the doctor reported, adding, "There was a time when there was no blood pressure and no pulse. But we kept giving her blood transfusions until the blood pressure returned and the pulse began."

Arvella and I always wanted our daughters to be responsible decision makers; not puppets. Our prayer was that they would not be indoctrinated, only inspired, independent possibility thinkers under the guidance of the

Holy Spirit. We had succeeded beyond our wildest dreams.

We were half a world away as Carol lay on the surgical table. Alone she faced a strange surgeon under glaring lights. Alone she heard him say, ''Carol, we might have to take your leg.'' What ran through her mind? Images of her horse—her softball games—her running—her skiing?

''You've got to be kidding.''

''We don't kid about things like that.''

She wept for a moment then quietly and bravely said, ''Do what you need to, doctor. Just make sure I get the best fake leg you can find!'' We would see this same brave spirit in her again and again the next days and weeks. She drew strength from the slogans that are so much a part of my ministry. And she proved to me they were greater than I had ever realized!

THERE IS NO GAIN WITHOUT PAIN

WHEN THE GOING GETS TOUGH, THE TOUGH GET GOING

LOOK AT WHAT YOU HAVE LEFT, NOT AT WHAT YOU HAVE LOST

I remember telling her that first afternoon, after she awakened, ''Carol, probably your greatest battle will be the battle to not feel sorry for yourself. Watch out for your greatest enemy—self pity!''

Her eyes flashed and with an amazingly strong voice she said, ''Don't worry about that, Dad. I've got enough problems right now without adding self pity to the pile!''

The diary I kept as I sat at her bedside through the long hours that faded into a haze of days and weeks, and then months, later reminded me of how close we all were walking with Christ, and how He brought His own sweet light into those long, dark nights.

9

God is So Good!

⟨◆⦙◆⟩

ARVELLA'S DIARY
Sunday a.m.
Carol's bedside
Sioux City, Iowa
July 9

It's morning again and all is quiet. In the distance I hear church bells ringing. It's Sunday morning and I am alone with Carol, except for the nurse who silently and efficiently checks Carol's vital signs ever so often.

Bob has gone to bed. Earlier he had taken the girls and Jim, Sheila's fiance, to find some motel rooms for us all. But there was no motel vacany in all of Sioux City, so the girls and Jim went home with relatives. The Sister who is supervising today kindly showed Bob a room here in the hospital that we could use during these critical days. How comforting that is, for both of us will be having problems with jet lag and we can just take shorter shifts this way. For we want to be at Carol's bedside every possible moment.

Carol is heavily sedated and is quiet except for a violent jerk ever so often, which shakes the bed and makes her wince with pain. Then her eyes fearfully search the room and immediately relax when I reassure her that I am here and everything will be all right. She drifts back to sleep.

I find myself silently praising God that He has spared her life, as I sense that I am playing a small part along with many others in the unfolding of a miracle. There are two small abrasions on her chin, and the nurse remarked, "They are from her helmet. How lucky she is that she was wearing her helmet. We see so many concussions and brain injuries from motorcycle accidents when helmets are not worn. If they live, many remain brain damaged." Miracle #1.

Carol remains very groggy but begins to wake up every ten to fifteen minutes to ask about when the Hour of Power would be on TV. She doesn't want to miss it. Finally at 10:00 a.m., she awakens to hear her daddy say, "This is the day that the Lord has made, we will rejoice and be glad in it." There is a weak smile and she is asleep again, but awakens enough during the message to hear the theme: "Rechoicing for Rejoicing." Her lips repeat the words slowly and she drops off to sleep.

Silently I look at her broken body and think, "O Carol, there will need to be a lot of re-choicing for you and for our family, but God is so good. You have a future with hope."

11:30 a.m.—Bob comes in to relieve me and I am so fatigued I think I could sleep standing up. A kind nurse ushers me through the empty chapel and up an elevator and there is a darkened bedroom, so cool and inviting. What a relief to shed the clothes I had worn for over twenty-four hours, shower, and then stretch out full length between the sheets . . . and sleep . . . .

Two hours later I am wide awake. I turn over. Surely I can use another hour of sleep, but it's no use. So I go back to Carol's bedside to find that Bob is ready for sleep again. It seems like two hour shifts will do very nicely for now. Again I breathe a silent thank you to God for the Sister who made such comforting accommodations available to us. God is so good!

Back at Carol's bedside, I watch as she continues her awake-asleep condition. Awake for a moment, Carol asks, "Will my fake foot have toes?" I marvel at how Carol is already accepting her loss and is focusing on the solution. I answer, "I don't know, Carol. I haven't seen a fake foot without the shoe. We will have a lot to learn about that. But we will get you the prettiest one we can." With that assurance she is asleep again, her pain controlled by heavy sedation.

Telephone calls are coming in for us now from across the nation. Bob Jr. called from New York. He had just arrived from London where he heard the news of Carol's accident. He is so concerned and anxious about her, and he will try to come to Iowa.

Earlier, during Bob's shift, Angie, one of Carol's friends from school and a member of her softball team, had read about the accident in the Sunday morning paper, and had called to talk to Carol to see if it really was true. When Bob had to tell her that Carol couldn't talk on the phone for a couple of days at least, he had to calm Angie down. She was so upset.

My thoughts were interrupted as the doctor came in and said he wanted to examine Carol and then would want to confer with us. "Would you please awaken Mr. Schuller? I would like to speak with both of you." His voice sounded quiet, but determined and concerned. Quickly I went to awaken Bob and in a little while the three of us met in a corridor outside the Intensive Care Unit. He introduced himself and then said—and I shall *never* forget his words, "You are fortunate to have your daughter. Surgery had to be delayed Friday night when she came in, because she went into extreme shock. There was no blood pressure, no pulse. *We thought she was gone!''*

My knees became like water but I kept my attention on what he was saying. I heard him explain why they had to amputate, and that he was very doubtful that the rest of her leg could be saved. They would be taking Carol back into surgery on Tuesday morning and would determine then if there would be any more amputation.

The rest of the day became a blur—a blur of relatives, getting a bite to eat in the cafeteria, talking with more relatives. Then my mother came and brought Gretchen.

Gretchen, looking bewildered, but very much loved by uncles and aunts, wanted to stay with us at the hospital. For a little while I had to forget everyone else, including Carol, and just hold and love Gretchen. She was hurting in her own way for her sister. I was told that Gretchen had fainted when she was taken to see Carol on Saturday.

As I held her on my lap in the cafeteria she began to tell me of the fun she was having on the farm. Then I said, ''Gretchen, I need you now more than ever before to be grownup. You must go along with Grandma to stay with Ross, Norm and Leah on the farm for tonight and tomorrow. Then maybe I'll send you back home to California with Sheila.'' This satisfied her. She kissed me and off she went with Grandma.

Sunday evening, alone again at Carol's bedside, I began to sort out my thinking. All the relatives had left. Sheila, Jeanne and Jim had gone home with them again and were going to make travel arrangements. Sheila and Jim were going back to California and Jeanne back to school. Bob was sleeping. The entire Intensive Care Ward was quiet with the exception of the nurses silently monitoring their patients.

I stood at Carol's bedside . . . alone and tired. I had only slept two hours since leaving Korea, yet I felt a strength and endurance beyond my own, and I am grateful. In my mind I heard again the words of a relative, ''The motorcycle is a tangled mass of steel . . . crushed between two cars. No one killed—Carol was the most critically injured. Carol's leg was mangled by the oncoming car. She was literally torn from the bike and landed in a ditch eighty-seven feet away.

Then I hear again the surgeon's words, ''No blood pressure, no pulse. We thought she was gone.'' But there she was alive. Under oxygen, yes, but she was alive.

Again, I heard the surgeon say, ''I decided to take a chance and not amputate the thigh—I doubt whether we can save it but for the time being she has her knee.''

We were experiencing miracle after miracle: Miracle #1—she wore a helmet. Miracle #2—the doctors saved her life. Miracle #3—she had her knee. Miracle #4—we had arrived safely and the entire family was now at her bedside except Bob, Jr., who was on his way. Miracle #5—the strength and energy that Bob and I both were experiencing was far beyond normal for us. We should be collapsing from jet lag and no rest, but we feel an invisible force upholding us, comforting us, sustaining us.

Miracle after precious miracle is made possible by the hundreds of people praying us through.

Like a precious string of pearls, there was a uniting bond of love and faith interceding for us to our Heavenly Father. And standing there, my heart overflowed with the presence of God in that hospital room.

10
Pearl-Producing Prayers

࿐

BOB'S DIARY
Monday Morning
Sioux City, Iowa
July 10

It's 3:15 a.m. I came to relieve Arvella at midnight. I slept from 9:15 to 11:15 and feel refreshed. I look at Carol and think, "Carol, you are doing great." Her positive attitude leaves me awestruck. I am amazed—mystified. She is not the Carol we know. She is too controlled, too cool and collected. Not once have I seen her come unglued emotionally. She is quiet, asks many questions, but has a sense of sincere acceptance. There seems to be no struggle, no resistance to what has happened."

"I tell myself, "She is thirteen" and suspect I am making a mistake. She is our 4th child born on the 4th of December in '64. I double check again. Yes, she is only thirteen. But she has the maturity of a young doctor who coolly and calculatingly reviews frankly and calmly the situation, demanding politely a briefing.

I've just read Arvella's diary, where she begins to count the miracles we are beginning to experience. I didn't have a chance to share with Arvella what the assisting doctor from Sioux Center told me when he came to see Carol today. He was so kind. "Carol asked me for pain relief when she came into the Sioux Center emergency room, but I said, 'Carol, it would further depress you. I must not.' So she accepted and patiently and very quietly tolerated the pain which was very, very intense. I don't tell you that to comfort you, but I cannot recall any patient ever so strong. *You can be very proud* of your daughter!"

He rode with Carol the sixty miles to the Sioux City hospital, and verified the shocking words we heard the surgeon say this afternoon, "She lived after losing most of her blood! We had to give her thirteen to fourteen units before surgery could begin."

Carol is running a fever now, so the nurse puts wet cloths with ice on her forehead. She groans and says, "My heel hurts, can you rub some lotion on it, Daddy?" I take a towel, roll it up, put it under the hollow between the heel and ankle, so that the heel is lifted from the bed.

"Carol," (for a moment I choke and my voice almost breaks, but I manage to keep from crying), "Mom and I will give you all the help we can, and you give all the help you can and God will work with us. God never works alone. He always chooses others and plans His miracles to use persons . . . often some whom we never know! Carol, every drop of your blood is from someone else . . . your own body's blood drained out in the ditch mostly, and the rest on the way to the hospital, but God had His miracle waiting for you through many, many people."

Carol is quiet again, so in the dimly lighted room I look at her white face against the white sheets and begin to pray silently, but with intensity, a prayer for her healing. I try to visualize healing. I try to repeat in technique the two-way prayer . . . visualizing healing. But *God* is saying to me:

"*No* miracle can be carbon copied or it becomes a human manipulation, not a divine miracle!"

Seek me!

Search me!

Trust me!

I am performing a miracle now . . . I can and will perform miracles of healing in Carol's mind, soul and body . . .

Believe me!

Let ME plan it . . . and unfold it! Thank you for your faith . . . ."

That's my message from the FATHER now, at 3:25 a.m., Monday, July 10, 1978!

I sense the presence of God so strongly now in this room, and I sense an extraordinary strength and comfort our family is receiving and I know that this, too, is a miracle because of all the prayers that are being said for Carol and us.

I shudder to think about how difficult it would have been if Carol's accident had happened a few days before when Arvella and I were in Kwang Chow, China, where the Communist guide kept on repeating, "No one believes anymore." How desolate and depressing the mood was there. Arvella and I and our traveling companions all responded the same way.

But thank God we were in Korea where we were surrounded with believing, praying Christian brothers and sisters. How they inspired me morning and evening as they responded so enthusiastically to my positive messages . . . 10,000 people saying, "Amen" all together, or all laughing together. They were the most responsive audience I have ever spoken to. And I felt such love and acceptance from them even though I was a stranger who did not even speak their language.

Dr. Cho said they (all 50,000 members of his church meeting at four services) would be praying for Carol. Then, as we landed in Los Angeles, I was told that our members and friends from Garden Grove Community Church (8,000 strong) were praying for Carol. And today, telephone calls and messages were received from across America. Churches are upholding us in prayer, Billy Graham had called, as did Oral Roberts.

I am amazed by a specific prayer that has already been answered. Arvella urgently asked everyone in Korea to pray specifically that Carol's knee would be spared. Now that we are here with Carol, one of the first things Carol said was, "I prayed I could keep my knee." And in California, Sheila said, "The prayer I kept praying was, "Lord, let Carol keep her knee, please!" Today, the assistant doctor reported, "Most surgeons would have removed her entire leg because her thigh is severely damaged, but the surgeon took a chance and amputated below the knee . . . . "

My heart is full of thanks again as I look at Carol, who is stirring, and think about what she said to Arvella last night. About 10:00 p.m. Arvella was trying to give Carol a sense of being at home, so she said, "Carol, it's 10:00—bedtime. Have you said your prayers already?" Carol's reply was a direct one: *"I haven't stopped praying!"*

From Korea, Garden Grove, and across America people were praying, and their prayers, intense with faith and believing, were producing pearl after pearl of precious miracles for our Carol.

5:35 a.m.—Carol was sleeping peacefully, but then she jerks awake. "Dream?" I ask, "Yes," she answers. "What about?" "We were in gymnastics running, then flipping with hand stands . . . it was my turn and I chickened out . . . that's when I woke up with a jerk."

"Carol, it's now the morning of the third day after your accident, you surely have improved over the past twenty-four hours since Mom and I came here."

"Gosh, I really am a lot better!" she offered enthusiastically, adding, "I know who to blame . . . I mean, give credit for that!"

"Then say it, pray it," I offered. She prayed, "Thank You, God, for saving my life . . . I know I almost died in the ditch. I kept repeating Your Twenty-Third Psalm, 'Though I walk through the valley of the shadow of death, You are with me,' I know you have a plan for my life and I will do it. I just thank you. Amen."

5:45 a.m.—She asks for her 6:00 a.m. shot. At 6:30 she gets ready for a dressing change. "It hurts really bad when they change dressings." "How do you handle that?" I ask. She answers, "I pray, 'Jesus don't let the pain be so bad. *Jesus, You be my Reliever.*' "

It takes only a few minutes to change the dressing and when I came back in the room, she says, "I did it." "What?" I ask. "I kept saying, 'Alleluia, You are my Reliever, Jesus,' and I only raised my voice for a second when they first raised my leg . . . *It worked!*"

"Carol, I'm having a wonderful time growing in my faith and love of God as I sit here and watch you and listen to you. Next fall I'm going to have a wonderful season of ministry because you are affirming everything I teach and preach. You illustrate how a positive attitude makes the difference between night and day . . . between heaven and hell!"

She listened and then asked, "Are you going to preach a sermon on *'God is our Reliever?'* " I answer, "Yes, that's a great idea." She is pleased and now the hypo is working and she drifts off to sleep.

11
"It Won't Change God's Plan for My Life"

~◦❁◦~

ARVELLA'S DIARY
Monday
July 10

"One of us will be with you at all times!"

This was our promise to Carol early this morning, when Bob and I changed shifts. "I'm going to bed awhile, Mom will be with you," were her daddy's words. What a comfort—a healing comfort this is to her. It gives meaning to God's promise:

"Fear not! When you go through the waters, I will be with you. And the fire, it shall not consume you, for I am your god! I have redeemed you! I know your name! I will be with you."

I've had a good sleep and a good cry. Each time I've gone to bed the hot tears have washed me inside and out. Quickly there is relief followed by sleep. And then no tears as I see Carol again. I feel relaxed, refreshed and in control of my emotions.

Carol is awakened by the nurse, for the checking of her vital signs.

"Forty eight, I'm going to be great!
Eighteen, I'm going to be keen!"
"What did you say, Carol?" I ask.
"Forty eight, I'm going to be great!
"   Eighteen, I'm going to be keen!"

My first reaction is that she is hallucinating, but I see her face almost break into a smile, and she says, See my traction Mom. There is a number 48 and over here is an 18." I look and look before I find the numbers on the knob of her traction. I am amazed and pleased, so we repeat the little rhyme again:

"Forty eight, I'm going to be great!
Eighteen, I'm going to be keen!"

And in guilt, I remember the many times I've complained over a minor disappointment in my life.

Carol seems to be sleeping, but then her eyes open and she asks the question, "What did they do with my leg?" Taken aback, I quickly recover and reply, "I signed a paper yesterday to have it buried." I waited for an outburst of tears, but instead her answer came back, "Good, I'm glad they didn't give it to me to take home in a jar like an appendix."

I gulped, but smiled and weakly replied that I was glad too. Two times this morning she has had a quick sense of humor. How good that is for the healing process. Another one of God's miracles.

Carol's eyes are closed now, but as the intercom comes on in the hallway, the hospital chaplain greets everyone, and then offers a morning prayer, concluding with the Lord's Prayer. I watch Carol's lips form the words,

"Thy will be done on earth as it is in Heaven."

8:30 a.m.—Carol seems so feverish; seems very concerned about her leg. It feels asleep, then it feels like a railroad train is going through her leg to the foot and toes that are no longer there. Phantom pains?!? I had heard about them. What other sensations will she experience? She is chilled now, and asks me to "tuck her in." How often I have "tucked her in," but now it is a special moment and I tuck her under her sheet and stroke her hair ever so gently . . . and she dozes off.

At 11:10 the doctor calls. He is concerned about Carol's temperature. It has gone up, but it could be the result of surgery. Tomorrow, Tuesday, at 1:30 p.m., Carol will go back into surgery and the decision will be made about her thigh. We will need to be present to sign giving permission for more amputation.

Apparently when she was thrown into the ditch her bone broke through the flesh of her thigh and plowed into the dirt. The surgeon spent a great deal time in surgery cleaning out her mangled thigh, but if I heard him correctly, he was certain that there was still far too much debris inside her broken and damaged thigh. I realize now that the battle to save her knee and thigh is crucial. Thank God that so many people everywhere are praying.

1:45 p.m.—Bob is asked to sign for further amputation in surgery tomorrow. He felt badly as he put his name on the paper. "I feel as if I lack faith— I've got to pray it through—God will surprise us all and I must believe that the doctor will say, "It wasn't necessary . . . ."

We are both at Carol's bedside and Carol remarks, "I'm concerned about my temperature. That's the only thing that's not going right. I'm drinking fluids to help it.''

Bob tells Carol to visualize pink tissue on her wounded thigh. "Why pink?" she asks. "That means flesh is getting blood and is alive," Bob answers.

Carol pauses . . . and then says:

WELL, I KNOW ONE THING—IF I NEED MORE AMPUTATION, IT WON'T CHANGE GOD'S PLAN FOR ME!''

We both silently gulp! Wow, that's positive faith at its best!

12

Guardian Angels

✥

BOB'S DIARY
Monday Afternoon
July 10

It's been a day of highs and lows, intense pain and blessed relief with pain relieving drugs, a day of wondering and belief; doubt and faith.

Will Carol be able to keep the rest of her leg? Her temperature rises, then tapers off. She continues to have strange sensations in her thigh. Is it from the swelling caused by the infection?

The entire family is here now except Bob, Jr., who cannot get plane reservations. He will be here tomorrow before Carol goes to surgery for the second time.

Telephone calls and telegrams are pouring in from all over the country. What a comfort these messages are. As we read Carol the names of her friends, she opens her eyes and listens intently, then smiles. It helps her to know she is not forgotten, but that she is important to those in her world.

I was called from Carol's bedside to the telephone. It is Cory SerVaas. I was shaking as I hung up. Cory, a medical doctor and editor of *The Saturday Evening Post*, had just given me incredible information.

"Bob, I just heard about Carol. And I must tell you that I just finished writing an article about a surgery that is now being done where severed limbs are sewn on again. You must get Carol to a replantation center."

"What's that and where do we go?" I replied.

"Replantation centers are special medical research centers where microvascular surgery is done. It is performed through the use of special microscopes and surgeons can repair the tiniest of blood vessels." Cory's voice continued over the wires, "There are four centers that I know about! There's one in Kentucky; Mayo Clinic in Rochester; Iowa city, Iowa, and one at your doorstep in California at the University of Southern California at Irvine.

"Cory," I respond, "Carol goes back to surgery tomorrow and we have already given consent for more amputation. How do I go about making arrangements to move Carol to one of these centers?"

"I'll do some telephoning, and get some information back to you immediately," was her urgent response.

God is at work—I feel it so strongly now!

There is a telephone call now from California. The Dean of the UCI Medical Center is on the line. Arvella takes the call. She comes back to report that he asked many questions. Where was Sioux City, Iowa? How far was it to Iowa City, Iowa? How far to Mayo Clinic, Rochester? Is Carol able to be moved? He offered to telephone Carol's surgeon and personally discuss Carol's condition with him.

I stay at Carol's bedside as Arvella waits by the telephone. Carol dozes off then awakens again. She asks, "What time is it? Will I be able to make the trip home? I am anxious to go home, but I'm scared. I'm scared of being moved. It hurts so much when they need to move me."

I reassure her that we won't move her unless the doctor feels it will be all right. We want to do only what is best for her. With that reassurance she dozes off again.

Sheila comes in to be with Carol, whispering that Arvella has to talk with me.

I meet Arvella in the crowded family room, and oblivious of others, try to read her expression. How tired she looks—naturally—she had been awake since early this morning and both of us are fighting jet lag from the continuous twenty-two hour flight from Korea. "Good news!" she reported, "The doctor has spoken with Dr. Van den Noort from UCI, and has agreed to come in and prepare Carol for the flight. An ambulance jet with a special intensive care nurse aboard will be flying in from Long Beach— arriving here at midnight. It will refuel and fly us all back to Orange County Airport. There an ambulance will take Carol directly to the Children's Hospital where a team of doctors will be waiting for us."

"That's good news," I breathlessly reply, sighing with a tremendous feeling of relief. Somehow, knowing we would be home would make everything so much easier to cope with.

Arvella continued, "I telephoned our relatives to see if they can possibly get Gretchen here. There is room on the plane for all of us, and Gretchen would be upset if we left her behind. I've got to eat something now, I've had virtually nothing all day and I'm feeling faint.''

With my eyes brimming with tears of gratitude over the miracle I see unfolding before me, I urge Arvella to go with Jeanne while I make my way back to Carol's bedside. God's plan is overwhelming as I ponder all that has happened in the last couple of hours—truly the result of many prayers being said for our Carol and for all of our family.

"God moves in a mysterious way, His wonders to perform!"

My heart jumps for joy as I look at Carol's still body. I wanted to shout "Carol, we're going home! We're going home!"

The news spread fast to all of the uncles, aunts and cousins. Soon the family room was filled with our loved ones. A high point in the summertime is a family reunion where we have such a wonderful time seeing brothers, sisters, nephews, nieces, cousins. Knowing there would not be the usual reunion, they came to wish us well; to reassure us of their prayers and to hold us up in our time of need. What a beautiful institution the family is. We drew strength from them as we looked into their faces and listened to their voices. One by one they tiptoed in to see Carol, and more than one relative returned to the family room crying quietly.

We were interrupted by Carol's doctor saying that he needed to prepare Carol for her trip. She would be put into a splint which would allow her to be moved with the least amount of pain. And then his voice and face brightened into the first and only smile we saw from him as he said, "I've checked her vital signs and they are much improved over this morning. I think it is because she knows she is going home to California." He expressed some concern over such a trip, especially because she was still receiving blood transfusions, but we were relieved and joyous at his optimistic report.

Soon after, the ambulance attendants came with a stretcher on wheels and Carol was gently and carefully placed on it and tied down to keep her from moving too much.

We were asked to stay in the family room during Carol's preparation for the trip, but occasionally we could hear a yell of pain, then a long groan. We all knew where those heart-rending cries were coming from, so our conversation became a little louder and busier to hopefully relieve us all from our helpless feelings.

Then, without warning, we saw the attendants roll Carol down the hall of the Intensive Care Unit toward the opposite direction from the family room. Jeanne was the first to notice and began to cry, "Carol is going and I won't get a chance to say good-bye to her." Jeanne was leaving for Israel the following morning for her summer of study. She was reluctant to go now because she wanted to stay with Carol and be at home with her family. But earlier in the day, Arvella and I both urged her to continue with her plans. There would be little for her to do during Carol's long weeks of healing in the hospital. So, reassured, she had decided to continue with her college studies in Jerusalem.

I ran to Jeanne, and putting my arms around her, said, "Of course, you will be able to say good-bye to Carol. In fact, you can ride in the ambulance with Carol to the airport." Calm now, Jeanne held my hands as the entire entourage of loving and concerned relatives followed.

Gretchen had not arrived yet—could we—should we hold up the flight for her? But as Carol was lifted into the ambulance, we saw car lights coming toward us and Gretchen bounced out of the car into her mom's arms. Suitcases were piled into different cars; ours still unpacked from Korea, Gretchen's, Carol's, Jim and Sheila's . . . there surely would be items left behind, but that was totally unimportant now.

A silent but loving caravan followed the ambulance through the still and almost empty streets toward the airport. There was a mood now of almost a celebration. Carol's nurse, whose hours of duty ended at 11:00 p.m., volunteered to go with Carol to the plane and personally hand over all the charts and orders to the special intensive care nurse accompanying Carol on the flight. Tenderly and delicately, she watched over Carol, checking her vital signs and watching for any unusual actions from Carol. How dedicated these people are . . . God's guardian angels . . . the doctors who worked over Carol for over seven hours through that first night, the nurses, the ambulance attendants . . . .

The airport is dark and deserted, except for a small room where we could wait. The fuel trucker and the airport night manager are the only other individuals waiting. Together we listen for the hum of the jet in the starry and quiet country night sky. Then we hear it and watch it come in like a bullet, and once on the ground, we watch it taxi to us with its long silver nose stretching out into the darkness.

There were now joyous goodbyes as each uncle and aunt said good-bye to Carol. Jeanne appeared relaxed and satisfied, having been with Carol until the plane doors were closed. There were no tears from her now. She was ready to study knowing that everything was going to be all right with her family. Soon after, we were sky bound. We were hungry, tremendously fatigued, scared, but much relieved and encouraged because we were on our way home, and our Carol was alive and we were together!

13
We Did It!

❦◎❦

ARVELLA'S DIARY
Tuesday A.M.
July 11

It was sometime in the wee hours of the morning—2:00 a.m.? 3:00 a.m.? 4:00 a.m.?—when we touched ground in Orange County.

I was surprised that I could function as well as I did—in spite of the weariness and confusion of time. It seemed now that an eternity had passed since we received the tragic phone call in Korea, and I had had so few hours of sleep since then. Surely my strength was not my own, but a direct result of all the prayers that were being said for us.

The flight was far more difficult than I had expected. Carol insisted I sit by her to hold her hand, and on the other side Gretchen, fast asleep, sat with her head leaning against my shoulder. Underneath my feet were two large containers of oxygen, should it be needed to replace the unit Carol was using. The plane, with its delicate and loving load, left no room to move about, so we were content to remain seated in small areas and make the most of it. We were so grateful that we would *very soon* be home.

But deep down I had a gnawing and growing fear. An odor, coming from Carol's leg, was nauseating me and it took all the positive thinking I could manage to keep from becoming physically ill. I did not dare to think, much less voice aloud, the horrible fear inside of me. Was Carol going to lose the rest of her leg? Was our rapid trip through the night sky all in vain? I shuddered and asked for a cup of coffee. Then I turned my attention to making Carol as comfortable as we could. She was so hot and feverish, in spite of the ice and ice water we gave her.

She asked if I could give her a back rub, since the nurse couldn't reach her back from where she was seated. I reached for the plastic bag that had come from the hospital with her belongings, and as I put my hand inside to get the lotion, I pulled out one dirty crumpled sock.

Curiously, I said to Carol, "Is this all you have left of the clothes you were wearing, Carol?" Silently, she nodded her head and then quietly and slowly said, "Mom, you're going to be mad at me!" I waited . . .! "I was wearing my new velour jacket, the one you said I could wear only to church or to dress up, and its all ruined. They had to cut it off me. Also," she paused, "I was wearing my best jeans, and my new Nike shoes."

I found myself at a loss for words, and muttered something like, "Oh well, you probably grew so much this summer, they would be too small for you anyway." Then I pulled out the lotion and very carefully and cautiously tried to rub her back where it hurt. There was no room for my hand between her hot back and the hard stretcher, and to avoid the large areas of raw flesh where the skin had been peeled off, much like a banana is peeled, was no small job. But the grateful smile of relief that crossed over her face was an unforgettable reward; and she fell off to sleep for a little while.

Finally, we saw the lights of Orange County, made our approach and landed. As we were taxiing, we saw some car lights; the ambulance and three other cars. Bob Jr. and his wife, Linda, bless them, had come along with two friends who had helped make the arrangements for the airplane.

Suddenly we felt the fresh air, then the embraces. I said a quick goodbye to Gretchen, telling her again that I was so proud of her for being so grown up. She would go home to Sheila's apartment and sleep; then later in the day go to Bob and Linda's home where she would "help" take care of their little four-month-old baby, Angie.

Carol was so excited about seeing her big brother, Bob. He was always so special to her. I remembered how when he was on the high school wrestling team, he would encourage Carol, who was then about five years old, to hit him in his stomach as hard as she could with her fists. There he would stand, upright, erect, not flinching a muscle, while she beat on him until her strength gave out. Then he would laugh at her and with her.

Now, there was no picking her up, nor any rough play, only a gentle kiss and touch of the hand. But his eyes held the wondering look of the question . . . Why Carol? Why our athlete, our energy bomb? Why Carol?

Linda stood by, helplessly, crying a little. How good it was to have them welcome us. The love that flowed again and again in all of our reunions with our family was such a source of strength to each of us. I could sense and feel it so strongly.

Quickly and carefully, Carol was carried into the ambulance and twenty minutes later we turned off the freeway and were greeted by the lighted sign with the familiar teddy bear symbol of the Children's Hospital. This would be Carol's home for the next few weeks? How long we did not know, but the teddy bear was a comforting greeting, reassuring me that Carol would be loved and cared for here.

In the emergency room, there were the forms to fill out. I was like a robot, without feeling. Meanwhile, Carol was ushered to her room on the special care floor—room 205. There, waiting for her was a team of three doctors; one a resident orthopedic physician; another, the orthopedic surgeon from the University of California at Irvine; and the third a plastic surgeon, also from the university. Bob was waiting for me outside of her room, and reported, "Carol's first words when they put her on the bed were 'I'm glad I'm home.' "

Soon after, the team of physicians came to us, their first words were—*"The doctors in Sioux City did a heroic job in saving her life!"*

The doctors continued, "We are very concerned about the odor. We hope it is just her front line bandages. But you will need to sign to give permission for possible amputation."

Our hearts sank into hopelessness. We had tried so hard to save the knee and thigh. Now, after the long tiring flight, would she still lose it? There was nothing to do but wearily put Carol into the hands of her heavenly Father. There was nothing we could do but pray and wait, and to comfort Carol as she waited for surgery.

Her pain is excruciating now with the splint digging into the top of her thigh. She is having ghost pains. Finally, after many tears, Carol is able to give the nurses directions to make her more comfortable.

Her bottom is so sore. She says, "Someone should invent a 'butt massage' ". My answer to her is, "Carol, maybe you can do that. Many people would love you for that!" She calms down and the nurse reminds her to keep her oxygen mask on.

Then the call comes from surgery. And the three of us hold hands and thank God for the wonderful doctors that are helping Carol. We affirm together that her knee and thigh can be saved because God is a God of miracles. And we end by thanking God for His love to all of us, especially Carol, and ask God to go into surgery with Carol so she will not need to be afraid.

I'm relieved that she is going to surgery. Her suffering has been much too great. As the surgery room doors swing shut, Bob and I look at each other. It is already past breakfast, but neither of us cares for any food. We look for a comfortable chair or couch for our worn out bodies and a kind nurse directs us to a family room, near Carol's room, and even brings us two blankets and some pillows.

Having released Carol to God's gracious care, I quickly doze off, only to awaken as the surgeon, dressed in his green surgical garb and mask, is shaking Bob, and saying the beautiful words: "Carol came through surgery fine! We did NOT amputate her knee and thigh! It will be a long and hard fight, but for now she still has her leg! Try to get some rest, Carol will be in recovery for another hour. When she returns to her room, she will need you!''

Numbly, almost in disbelief, I shake myself awake. ''Thank You, God. Thank You, God!''

Now we are hungry, and so we wash our faces and eat some breakfast. And we are back in Carol's room as she comes from surgery.

She is under pain reliever, but so joyful, fully aware that for the second time her knee and her thigh have been saved.

''We did it, Dad!''

''We did it!'' was her jubilant and victorious salutation.

''We did it'' . . .yes, *we* did it. How big is that word, ''we''!

''We'' . . . God, the doctors, nurses, family, friends, thousands of people praying, working!— The lab technicians, the many people who donated blood, the people who built the hospitals, raised the funds, the researchers who developed the medicines, drugs—Some who helped recently, others many years ago—all included in the word, ''we''.

Together, WE DID IT!

14
Play it Down! Pray it Up!

BOB'S DIARY
July 12, Wednesday

It's Wednesday morning. I've had an early 4:00 a.m. breakfast with Arvella at Denny's, an all-night coffee shop. Arvella has gone home to bed. Carol had a distressing night. The traction was hurting so badly—"like a butcher knife cutting my leg off," was Carol's description.

Her nurse, after working most of the night just to make her comfortable, finally telephoned the orthopedic resident doctor. He came and made several adjustments on her traction to relieve her pain. But the phantom pains are so severe, "Oooh . . . my foot!" But the foot is no longer there. How do you relieve the pain of something that no longer exists?

Now, Carol is awake . . . blissful, serene and peaceful. I have quietly been sharing some morning devotions with her and she responds, "I'm getting sleepy but first I want you to say something." "Yes,

Carol, go ahead," I reply. "Dad, you have the best way of speaking and it's like you gave a message just for me without preparing for it. I love you, Dad."

Carol lifted her face and I put my lips to her hot face and feverish lips, and then she closed her eyes. What did I say to her? I'm trying to recall. I remember saying, "Carol, in two-way prayer, Jesus said to me, 'Tell Carol, I'm proud of her.'" I also shared how the Koreans prayed in their church to save her knee. So many, many, many people love her and pray for her. "Yes, Dad," she said, "I didn't know I had so many friends. Even kids from school I didn't think cared about me are calling Mom."

I shared with her how God does have a super special ministry for her as He told her in the Sioux City Hospital.

The doctor interrupts my thoughts and remarks that she is sleeping so peacefully and beautifully. He tells me "The first job is behind us—to save her life. Blood gases, for some reasons we don't know, tend to form with such fractures, and she had a problem. It affects the lungs but this is clearing up now.

"Our next step is to keep out infection and the danger of infection seems to be behind us. But if it happens again, then we fight it. The third step will be to close the wounds. So for now the wounds will reamin open to allow drainage of any possible infection from foreign matter that entered her thigh while she was in the ditch.

"Hopefully in a week her wounds can be closed, then the fracture can be lined up so her leg will heal properly for a prosthesis." He concluded, "She is doing very well! She is an unusual girl!"

Now reassured with the doctor's comments, I recall again the message that I'm sure came from

God while Arvella and I were enroute from Korea.

I recall how I was in the lavatory on the plane when the amazing sentence came into my mind, "Schuller, you're taking it too hard. 'Play it down and pray it up!' "

PLAY IT DOWN AND PRAY IT UP!

"Schuller, she didn't lose her life, she didn't lose her hand, she can still play the violin, she can still play the piano. She didn't lose both legs, only one. She's no embarrassment to her Lord, to her youth group, or to you! You're exaggerating it. Play it down! Play it down!"

I confess now that at first, this experience had the overtone, if not the reality, of the element of human tragedy. My first inclination was to exaggerate the tragic element. And as I look back on twenty-eight years as a pastor, I remembered talking to and praying for people in a variety of situations; parents who lost children; human tragedies with enormous heartbreak. In every instance the first inclination was to exaggerate the tragic element, because there is the reality of a tragedy in the situation. We know it's tough and because of this the normal safeguards that would keep us from exaggerating are probably down. So play it down, and pray it up! "God, how do I pray it up?" His answer was clear: "She is alive, thank me for that!"

Thank You, God, that she's alive!
Thank You, God, that she has her hands!
Thank You, God, that she still has another leg!
Thank You, God, that she has You as her friend!

The gift Arvella and I gave to Carol was paying off

now—the gift of faith she received because we insisted she go to Church school. Family devotions are a must in our house. We did not, as parents, agree with the popular attitude that children should be allowed to grow up and pick their own faith. That always seemed so wrong, so irresponsible, such a bad mistake.

When we were a half a world away, our thirteen-year-old daughter, out of the sound of our voices, was able to go to her spiritual bank and make a withdrawal from the scripture verses that she'd memorized in Sunday school, and that was worth more than $5,000 or $10,000 or $100,000 to both her and to me.

An immediate withdrawal! Even more valuable than education, nutrition, health or morality, was the gift of a vital faith we gave to Carol. For when the time came when we were too far from her to help and she needed it, her faith saw her through.

Play it down and pray it up!

"Thank You, God, You have taught me today that You are in control and when You are in control things aren't nearly so bad as I think they are. Continue to remind me to play it down and pray it up. My spirit is up. I know You are alive, because I know You as my friend as Carol knows You also.

"Thank You, God, for being the grand architect of the universe; the grand cosmic energy; the master mind who became the master heart through Jesus Christ. Thank You."

9:04—Carol has been awake and had a brief battle with pain. I was amazed to see her reach for the bar above her head to raise her body two inches off the bed. It helps to shift the pressure from some of the raw areas of her back. I praise her for her little victory and she replies with a smile, "I'm going to be able to water ski better than ever!

I continue to be amazed at her positive attitude and remarks. Only for awhile yesterday did she have a complaining negative attitude. Once she said, "I wish this hadn't happened!" And I gently, but I think wisely, rebuked her, "That thought did not come from Jesus. Don't ever say or think 'I wish it hadn't happened.' " She fell asleep as if that evil, negative spirit, verbalized in the sentence of futile regret, was gone by claiming Jesus as the author of only inspiring and positive thoughts.

Now Carol is asleep again, hands folded one on top of the other across her chest. There is a saintly sweetness that has cast an aura around her—like a halo. As I keep watch over her I feel drawn so close to Jesus.

15

Phantom Pains

ARVELLA'S DIARY
Wednesday Evening
July 12

How good to be home in Orange County. I wonder how often I've thought that since the plane touched ground in the wee hours yesterday morning. I no longer feel like the zombie I must have been yesterday, not having the opprotunity to change clothes for at least thirty hours or more. I never realized when I dressed early Monday morning in our room at Sioux City, Iowa, that circumstances and events would happen so fast.

I feel so refreshed now, even though I still must look like something from another planet with the little sleep I am getting. Our own bed felt so good and I did have a good cry to release all kinds of pent-up emotions, tears of fatigue physically and emotionally, tears of sorrow to see Carol hurting so much, but also tremendous tears of gratitude to God, that we still have her. As I see her broken and swollen body, I see it is a miracle that she survived and by the grace of Almighty God, Carol is alive.

My tears are also because I sensed a special nearness of the presence of God, not only at Carol's bedside, but here at home, in our bed, as I put my head on the pillow. It was as if Jesus had His loving arms around me too, comforting me and lifting me up.

How good it is to let go and just cry, and cry and cry, and then blessed, blessed sleep . . . .

Carol is receiving no more blood transfusions since after surgery and that looks encouraging. Her feverish hands and face still worry me—we must continue to pray that the infection will not invade the damaged area of her thigh.

It takes so little to comfort her. I have learned where the raw areas of her back are, and so I can, for a little while, give her relief as I rub the hospital lotion on her hot back. She sighs such a comfortable sigh. Then Carol asks me to massage the one foot she has. She gives me careful directions—''Underneath my toes. Now my heel. Now the top of the foot. Oh, that feels good. That's where it hurts on the foot that isn't there, and it helps so much if you rub the same place on the foot I have. Thanks, Mom.''

When I arrived back at the hospital this evening, Bob reported to me his conversation with the resident orthopedic doctor. Bob had asked him how long the phantom pains would last . . . a month? Six months? A year? Longer than that? His answer was, ''We never know, we don't really understand them, ... but probably not too long.''

That sounded hopeful. Then Bob asked him if hypnosis as a therapy had ever been used to eliminate the phantom pains. The doctor was not aware of this, but thought it could be quite helpful.

Surely prayer can and could heal her here!

Speaking of prayer, I wonder if the priest, "Father Mac," will be stopping by tonight. He has such a nice bedside manner. I am very impressed with him and I could tell that Carol liked him immediately. He stayed for such a brief time, and asked Carol if he could leave a blessing for her. Then he took her hands so very gently, and as she closed her eyes, he gave a brief prayer for God's comfort and peace through the night. I could tell that he really helped her.

I continue to be amazed at the beautiful way in which we are all being supported in prayer, especially Carol. I am awestruck at the story that our caretaker-gardener, Maurie, told me this afternoon.

Maurie was very upset about Carol. He seemed almost beside himself. He kept pacing back and forth through the kitchen, as he listened intently while I shared how Carol was hurt and what her condition was when I left her early this morning.

I recall how Maurie came to us as a displaced person about twenty-three years ago. We had sponsored him from Dutch Indonesia. He had been a prisoner of war for a number of years during World War II. He had been marked for death two times. When he came to us, he was like a whipped dog. He spoke little English and seemed happiest when he was around the children. He has loved our family and has been so devoted to all of us, especially the children. Now, Carol's accident was almost too much for him.

He continued his nervous pacing back and forth as he shared with me:

"I was awakened on Friday night from my sleep

with a frightening and very clear message 'Carol Schuller is dying!' The message was so strong that I got out of my bed and fell on my knees and prayed for Carol. The next morning I thought of it only as a bad dream, because then I thought 'Carol Schuller is not at home. Carol is in Iowa visiting her grandmother.' I did not know until it was announced in church—a day and a half later—that Carol was indeed in danger of losing her life and she needed my prayer.''

What a beautiful experience . . .

Carol isn't eating. Her dinner remains untouched on the tray. Her entire system has had such a shock. She seems to have a great deal of pain in the lower abdomen area. Her greatest injuries and stitches are all below her waistline. It seems as if her body was just ripped apart as she flew off the bike; however, I overheard her tell the nurse a little while ago that the car crunched her leg. She heard the crunch but there was no pain that she remembers at that time. It was in the ditch when the pain began to engulf her.

I ask her if she wants to say her evening prayers or wait until later. Carol gestures yes, with the nod of her head and her garbled voice quietly speaks through the oxygen mask, which has for the time being become a part of her attire. Other than that her body lies naked under a sheet, too sore for even a gown.

Her prayer is a long one and now as I write this much later in the night, I remember just a part of it . . .

"Dear Jesus,

Thank You for being my friend. Thank You that You will never leave me . . . Thank You for answering me yesterday in surgery. I asked You to save my

-66-

knee and heal it, and You did. Now I ask You again to heal my knee . . . and keep up the good work. I pray for my cousin, Mark, who also was hurt and for all my friends. Amen.''

Then, with hardly a pause, Carol said, "Mom, where is my Bible?" I replied, "It's right here on the table. It was in your hospital bag that came from the Sioux City hospital."

I did not know Carol had taken her Bible along to Iowa, for she packed her own suitcase. I was elated to know that the Bible was so meaningful to her.

Now she was giving me instructions:

"Would you get my Bible and turn to I Corinthians 13? That's my favorite chapter in the Bible and I have a letter there."

I picked up her Bible and yes, there was a folded letter between the pages exactly where she said it would be.

When I opened the folded page, my heart skipped a beat, for there was a letter dated:

Winter Camp 2/26/78

"Dear Jesus,

I know that a lot of this is going to be. . . I want this or want that. But it's also going to be thank you's. Well, I guess I'll start out with—thank You for being my friend and coming into my life—thank You for dying on the cross for me. I love You and—*please never leave me*. I'll write again soon.

Carol

I read the letter aloud to Carol and her only reply is, "I should write Jesus another letter but I've been too busy and it hurts so much . . ." I gently replied, "Jesus understands. He knows what pain is. You can write to Him as soon as you are able to sit up a little."

Now she drifts off to sleep, and again I am speechless over the beautiful way God has taken care of our Carol.

For each of our children, our hope and goal has been to so guide and lead them in their walk of faith, that when they reach the vulnerable and precarious years of junior high, they would make a commitment to their Lord to walk with Him and to ask God to plan and lead their lives. So our prayer through this past year had been for Carol to make a deep and meaningful decision to dedicate her life to Christ. We were not only praying, we were planning for that goal and that was the reason Carol was going to go to summer camp, scheduled two days after the accident. Hopefully, in our beautiful mountains with sensitive youth counselors to inspire her, she would have an opportunity for her commitment.

But my faith was too small. God had already planned Carol's decision time, for He knew she would need to be walking close to Him through these weeks of pain and tragedy.

My solitude is abruptly interrupted as Carol jerks violently and then begins to cry.

"What's wrong, Carol?" I asked. "I had a dream. I was kicking the ball and then I really kicked. . .

16
Our
Wounded Angel

࿐

BOB'S DIARY
Saturday, July 15
6:45 a.m.

I'm writing this, with wet eyes, as I sit alone at Carol's bed. Last night she had her third surgery. The operation lasted from 5:45 to 8:00 p.m. All day Friday, Carol had such discomfort. Her bath was so very painful.

Then she could have no food for the day. At breakfast, they came with Carol's favorite food—French toast. The girl bringing in the tray felt so badly. She hadn't been told that Carol was not to eat. The day was rough on all of us. Carol seemed to really be having some painful spasms throughout her lower abdomen area. The hours seemed to go so slowly.

When the doctor came in to see Carol, Arvella and I sensed more concern than usual in his attitude. He was very specific that we wait in Carol's room during surgery in cased he needed to see us. It upset Arvella but I reassured her that when I signed for surgery this time, there was no phrase included about "possible amputation." So I was optimistic, but I agreed that the surgeon seemed very grave.

It was a long, hard wait alone—just Arvella and I. We watched the afternoon sun drop behind the tall buildings on the west horizon, and the room became almost depressing as the evening dusk descended. What a relief to see "Father Mac," the chaplain, gently knock and then come to sit with us for a long time. He was a real "spirit-lifter" and "cheerer-upper." When he stood to leave he placed one hand on Arvella's head and one hand on mine as he prayed a prayer of blessing for Carol right now in surgery, and for strength for us as parents. The warm touch of his hand and his gentle voice brought a fresh presence of God into the room and I was greatly comforted. I think Arvella was too, because she began to cry softly—only for a minute though—for usually she is too reserved to cry.

Soon after, the doctor, wearing his green surgical gown and cap, and with his surgical mask pulled down below his chin, came briskly into the room and in a straight-forward manner began to tell us about the infection that had invaded both her injured thigh and knee. He explained a two pronged attack they were going to use to fight the infection by a team of specialists including an infectious disease specialist. Cultures taken during surgery would be grown and identified in order to determine the right antibiotic; also the wounds would be kept open and two tubes had been placed through the flesh to the knee and the femur to irrigate the infected area and flush out the bacteria.

Then after we asked a few questions, he looked at us with great intensity and carefully choosing his words, slowly said, "The question we also need to ask is, wouldn't it be easier for Carol to adjust to losing her complete leg than to have her go through the tremendous fight that is going to be so rough for the next weeks and possibly months. As a doctor I also have to ask how much can her body take?''

Knowing we had no answer, he gently suggested that we grab a bite to eat while Carol is in recovery, because she will be hurting badly tonight and we will want to be with her.

Numb and shaken nearly as badly as we were after the first telephone call in Korea, Arvella and I walk to the elevator, push the button to ''1'' and, like computerized robots, walk through the lobby crowded with evening visitors and on to the car to go eat.

We were so sure that if Carol were to lose her knee and thigh it would have been in the second surgery. We thought that threat was virtually behind us, but now the threat is serious and alarming.

''I can't eat, Arvella. I have no appetite,'' is my first attempt at conversation. Arvella answered, ''I'm not hungry either, but I really feel I have to eat something. Let's go home, though, for I don't want to be around people.''

Arvella tried to thaw out and grill a hamburger. It turned out rare, but she somehow managed to eat a part of it—no bun, no salad, just the hamburger alone on her plate. Then we rushed back to Carol's room and came through the doorway to find that she had just been wheeled back to her room. Three nurses were working on her, connecting and checking tubes leading to her leg. She was under oxygen again and above her hung the antibotics for the IV's and a plastic bag filled with a dark red substance. More blood, that must be over twenty-four pints she has had in all by now.

Our wounded angel, so white against the sheets . . . her lips as white as all the white around her. So often I had seen these same cheeks and lips rosy and flushed from playing ball, or returning from a long ride on Lady, her horse. Now the color was all gone. There was little response or movement from her. Yes, she was truly our wounded angel. Arvella and I stayed near her bedside, then I went home to hopefully sleep and later relieve Arvella in the early morning hours.

Still in a numbed state I arrived home and got into bed. . . not even putting a light on. I fell asleep only to awaken suddenly. What time was it? 2:30? 3:30?

In the dark, I prayed:

"Jesus, You have to be alive! We cannot do without You. Jesus, You have helped, You have healed . . ."

I cannot recall the rest of my prayer, except for a pledge promise I made to Him. It came as I visualized my beautiful Carol's saintly serene sweet, pure face on the pillow. Christ shows Himself through her so clearly. "Jesus, Carol has brought You so close to me. *I will never drift from You as long as I have Carol to love.*"

Has God chosen Carol to be my spiritual and moral and emotional guardian angel? I feel I am in the presence of a heavenly creature—an angelic being as I sit at her bedside. The presence of God? My stream of tears are turning into a string of pearls.

I showered, dressed and returned to the hospital. There is a large sign on the door—"Isolation," Arvella is wearing a gown. That's new! She looks so worn out that the nurse suggests that we go for a cup of coffee. We go to Denny's again for an early, early breakfast. Arvella has a hard time eating her breakfast because of her tears. She is ready to accept more amputation. Carol's night has been so bad; she can't stand to see Carol go through so much pain. I share my prayer time with her and give her hope, but it doesn't help much. She needs to rest, so I send her home, and I return to the bedside of my wounded angel.

I am again in tears. But now they are joy tears for I have opened the Bible to Job 42: It's the last chapter and the bottom line of the Living Bible translation:

"So the Lord blessed Job at the end of his life more than at the beginning . . . ." The blessing are listed. 14,000 sheep—6,000 camels. God also gave him seven more sons and three more daughters. The closing sentence is beautiful: *"Then at last he died an old, old man after living a long good life."*

I go back to read the opening lines of the last chapter, which is Job's confession of faith.

"I know that You can do anything and that no one can stop You . . ."

I pray and visualize purging and purification. Carol awakens and I share with her how we need to visualize the war that is being fought right now in her thigh and knee. "Visualize the army of Jesus as the pure blood cells winning over the bad bacteria Christ's army is moving forward but the army needs to be fed, so you need to eat and get strong, and His army needs someone to believe that Jesus' army will be the victorious one."

The crisis will be past in a week, at least that's my understanding. Then we will know if Carol will be spared more amputation.

The resident doctor comes in and seems very positive that they will be able to conquer the infection. Then he asked me to leave while he changes her bandages. I hear her cry of pain echo down the hallway, so I quickly push the elevator button to floor one. I am still concerned about Arvella so decide to drive home—only a ten minute drive—to see how she is. Quietly, I unlock the door and tiptoe to our bedroom. She is fast asleep, but her face is tear-stained against the wet pillow.

I tiptoe back to the kitchen, find a piece of paper I can use as a mini-poster and in big bold letters, I write:

GOOD NEWS!

CAROL MUCH BETTER!
SHE WILL BE O.K.
DR. VERY POSITIVE

I taped the paper to the hallway door frame so Arvella will be sure to see it.

Feeling up now, I return to Carol's bedside. She is calm again. A bath and a soothing back rub after the bandage change has helped her forget the pain, and now feeling comfortable and relaxed, she wants to share with me.

"Dad, I couldn't tell you last night, because I hurt too much. But on the way to surgery the doctors all looked so worried that I got scared. So I began to pray—not out loud, you know—in my mind. And I had two-way prayer. I asked God, 'Will I lose my leg?' He said, 'No!' I asked, 'Will I keep my knee?' God said, 'Yes.' When the nurses asked me if I was afraid, I said, '*No.*' I didn't tell them why, but it really helped to talk to God like that.

"And see! I have my knee and my thigh!"

Smiling at Carol, I think of the message I left for Arvella, "Good news! Carol is going to be O.K.!"

17

Good News!
Carol Will be OK!

❧◦⊙◦❧

ARVELLA WRITING

What a surge of hope and strength flowed through me as I spotted the white piece of paper taped in such an obvious place. As I quickly read the positive message I had to smile. This was so like Bob—always doing something for me in such an unusual and dramatic way.

I was ready to face a new day now with new hope and new energy because *Carol was going to be O.K.!* Bob had prayed it through and very early this morning I had prayed it through . . .*with my tears turning to pearls*. Now this was like a reassuring message from God.

There were very few entries written in our bedside diary after this. We began to realize that Carol's healing would come very slowly and her road back to an active life would be a long, lonely one. Our life style would change dramatically for the next weeks and months. There would be high times and low times; mountain-top experiences with our Lord, because people were praying for us, and deep valleys of pain and despair.

It was three weeks before suitcases were finally all unpacked. Carol's suitcase was the last one; I emptied it and it was difficult, for her clothes showed the wear and tear of an active girl. During the first week I only went home to sleep and perhaps do a washer-full of laundry. There was no food in the house and I didn't take the time to shop for groceries. It took less time to eat at the hospital-cafeteria, so we could spend as much time as possible with Carol. Few visitors were allowed because she was in isolation, but she did not care to see many anyway, because it demanded all her energy to cope with the pain and discomfort through the first weeks.

Could we get back to a normal life-style? We all needed a regular routine, but in these circumstances, how would we accomplish this?

Depression and frustration began to creep into my attitude and it became a new enemy for me to cope with. Again and again I would pray it through and receive the help and guidance from God—often times it came through a friend. God's little miracles day-by-day continued to come our way.

Carol learned how to cope with pain and we learned how to comfort her. For three weeks the bandages had to be changed three times daily, and the open raw flesh of her wounds were made to bleed to help the infection escape from the thigh and raw end of her mini-leg. Even to move, or to bump her traction, sent unbelievable shock waves of severe pain throughout her body. When fear of the pain would come even before the nurses or doctors would touch her, she learned that to repeat the name of "Jesus" over and over again—sometimes audible, most of the time inaudible—helped the most in the worst of her pain.

Television helped to take her mind away from the long hours of discomfort, as she learned to play the morning game shows. Our own program became a tremendous source of strength to her, and she became Daddy's valued critic—Sunday after Sunday.

Her tremendous interest in sports, and especially baseball, helped in her hours of pain. When the radio was tuned to her favorite team playing, she would appear to be asleep, but when one of her favorite players would hit a home run she would weakly raise a hand with the IV dangling from it, and put her thumb into the air. It became her way of rooting for her team and saying *"ALL RIGHT!"*

Her love of music helped tremendously also, as she listened over and over again to the same songs on her tape deck, a gift from a wonderful friend of hers. When the nights were rough and painful, she preferred the lights to be dimmed. Again and again we watched as the words of the music began to soothe, comfort and bring fresh courage to her sore and tired body.

"So, shine, shine on in the night
Shine, shine be a light . . . ."

They were beautiful positive messages that programmed her mind and her attitude to feel that God had not forgotten her. How can you help but "Shine in the night" when you hear the message strong and clear, hour after hour, night after night.

A friend wisely and kindly advised us to let Carol

know that we realized she was really hurting. He shared how when he went through a tremendous amount of pain in a situation similar to Carol's. He would become so angry when he told people he was hurting so badly and they would ignore his comment or change the subject.

So, when Carol would say, "Oh, I hurt, Mommy," or "It hurts, Daddy!" we learned to comfort her through stroking her uninjured leg—or her hair or face—the only parts of her body that were not hurting. And often we would say, "I know, I only wish I could hurt for you," and her immediate reaction would be, "Oh, no, I wouldn't want that."

About eight weeks after the accident the young resident doctor came in to remove the wire sutures that closed the end of her mini-leg. He told Carol it would hurt, but he didn't want to put her to sleep because she would be asleep and drowsy too long. He suggested that she grab tight to my hand. But that was not sufficient. With each twist of the wire Carol let go with the most blood-curdling cries I had ever heard from anyone. When the ordeal was over, in a tired and hoarse voice, she replied, "That hurt more than when I was in the ditch!" The young doctor felt badly and before he left her room, he took time to caress her hand and calm her down.

After he had left Carol turned her wornout body and tear-stained face to me and said weakly, "Mom, I wasn't faking it. It really hurt as much as in the ditch," and she began to cry softly.

Constraining myself no longer, I wept with her. I so wished I could bear her pain for her, but I could only stand by helplessly. I told her so and Carol replied through her tears, "No, Mom, I can take it much better than you. Never do I want you to go through that."

In all her hurting and pain, only once did I hear Carol remorsefully say, "Maybe it would have been better if I had died in the ditch."

But when the depression came, it came seldom and only for a moment, for she had the capacity to "turn her mental dial" to the bright side of her predicament. Not once do I recall even a twinge of resentment about the accident.

Her nightmares and phantom pains became less through the weeks following her accident. This was a tremendous blessing and relief, and was one more of God's many miracles. Often she had to relive, through nightmares, the feeling of her body flying through the air and being twisted and torn apart again and again.

A crash on a TV program or sirens on the street below the window of her hospital room sent her into uncontrollable hysteria. Our prayers became centered, not only on the healing of her body, but also on the healing of her memories.

Homesickness became a real problem and when we stopped staying nights with Carol, we promised her that she could telephone us whenever she needed or wanted to, and we could be at the hospital in just ten minutes.

It soon became a familiar routine to have the telephone awaken us anytime from 4:30 a.m. on. As Carol began to feel better the hour became later. Frequently she would be crying:

"I want to come home today."

"I want my own bed."

"I don't like it here anymore."

"I miss Gretchen."

"I want to go riding with Lady (her horse)."

"I want to go and run with Nicki (her dog)."

Carol then began to learn a prayer that is familiar to many adults, but was new to her. The prayer had tremendous power to calm her and completely change her mind. Over and over, day-in and day-out we would say:

"You cannot come home today, and let's just think about today—let's not try to solve tomorrow's problems. Just for today—repeat after me:

"Dear Lord, *help me to accept what cannot be changed!*"

Repeat it again:

"Help me to accept what I cannot change!"
To Accept what I
Cannot change!
To *accept!*
Accept!
Accept!

18
A
Family of Pearls

❧❀❧

ARVELLA WRITING

The shock of Carol's accident had a tremendous effect on the entire family. We all realized how close we came to losing her, and that only by the grace of God, and through His miracles, her life had been spared.

Each one reacted and responded in a different way. Gretchen, two years younger and constantly in Carol's shadow, had a lost feeling without her. Often we would find her in Carol's room, just looking at Carol's things or stroking one of Carol's stuffed animals.

One day, Gretchen summed up her feelings in an amazing, but truthful explanation to a little friend of hers who was spending the night; "I am so glad that you could stay with me tonight. I have been so lonesome without having Carol here to fight with me."

Bob and Linda, Sheila and Jim—all were so super. Bob and Linda—especially Linda—were so great with Gretchen, inviting her to stay overnight to "babysit" little Angie. That was such a treat for Gretchen. Then Linda took her shopping for her fall school clothes. There was so much love for her there. It helped so much. Then Sheila and Jim spent so much time writing and planning the hospital *Faith Prescriptions.** How great to see the family all pitching in to do their part. They kept in touch with Carol constantly, either visiting her to phoning her daily.

We heard each other say more than once that Carol's accident brought our family closer together and each one shared a new experience in prayer with God. Surely we all were closer to Him.

I can sum it up best by sharing a paper that our college student, Jeanne, wrote for her first assignment in Journalism for the fall term:

❧⊙⋈⊙❧

It was hot and dusty as I struggled to grasp the words of the Israeli tour guide who failed to communicate the importance of the mass of ruins we stood staring at. Eventually my thoughts could cling no longer to the history of the Herodian Palace. I found myself recalling the weekend prior to my flight to the Holy Land.

I was back at the campus of Wheaton College and had just arrived home from adventuring into the "windy city" with my roommate. The night was muggy and my breathing was heavy as I had to suck in the humid summer air. It was not as heavy as the

---

*You will find fixty-six of these *Faith Prescriptions* beginning on page 98.

blackness of the night, however, which seemed to bring a sense of awe and fear of what that night secretly held. I was tired though, and had no need of late nights or rude awakenings, so before retiring I reluctantly removed the phone from the hook above my dormitory bed. Even as I acted, the thought of emergency calls flashed quickly through my mind. I removed it anyway.

Had I imagined a rude awakening, it wouldn't have been as strong as the knock on my door that morning. I read seven a.m. on the clock as I stood groggily before my friend from the room across the hall. Her concerned eyes bothered me more than the news of a phone call for me in her room. Yet the added threat of it being an emergency unnerved me.

I was no longer tired, but startling awake as I picked up the phone and heard my sister's voice come through the merciless wires of the cold receiver. "Jeanne, I have horrible news . . .", she said bluntly. She started to cry and her voice trembled as she informed me of the accident my little sister had been in the night before. The black night had swallowed the perception of vision my cousin had as he drove the motorcycle with thirteen-year-old Carol clinging to his back. A car had stopped suddenly and another one appeared to shatter the plan to pass the parked vehicle. The bike and car hit, metal against metal, and flesh against asphalt. My sister was alive, but only after having bled painfully in a ditch as minutes ticked on, drawing the life-giving blood from her. Doctors had miraculously saved her life, but not the mangled calf of her left leg. The amputation had been immediate and final. The news was also final as my sister concluded her call.

I stood shocked, stunned by the fact that

God would allow what appeared to be a tragedy in the life of my family. After all, wasn't my father the internationally known pastor, who inspired millions Sunday after Sunday with his messages of Possibility Thinking and Self-Love? The family had always practiced this philosophy before, but now as this stared me in the face, I felt weak, and helpless, and wondered if God's plan for my sister's life was under control after all.

My immediate reactions were flustered. I clumsily retreated to my room to call for a flight to the small town in Iowa, where I imagined my sister lying dejected in a second-rate hospital room. After clearing my mind with a hot shower, I was able to phone close friends for prayer and support. Then I found myself on a small plane heading to my sister's side.

It was on that slow, time-consuming plane that God filled my spirit and began to speak. ''Turn your scars into stars,'' ''Every end is a new beginning,'' various sayings and verses flooded light on the dark cloud I had let cover the plan God had for my sister. Slowly I realized this was God's will and the love of the Creator for my sister was greater than mine. It was a long flight . . . but only as long as it took for my will to surrender to His, Who's plan was permanent.

The small aircraft touched lightly, and slowed cautiously in front of the compacted airport set neatly among the tall cornfields. I met my relatives at the gateway feeling unsure of what to do or say. I had arrived over eighteen hours after the accident, and yet I was the first of the immediate family to reach Carol's bedside. My parents were still enroute from Korea to Los Angeles, after they had suddenly left the Conference of Korean Churches which my father had been conducting.

Now I was only minutes from actually seeing my sister as I imagined her, bruised and maimed. I pictured her blonde silky hair, now knotted and bloody against a swollen, blue face. I imagined her once slender, sleek legs now unbalanced and torn. I saw her sparkling blue eyes now filled with tears, and her normal innocent smile puckered into a whimper. I saw her in pain. I felt her in pain.

Yet, when I walked into the cold, steel blue room where she lay amid a collage of machines, bars, tubes, and bandages, I saw no pain, and I felt no pain. Rather, I saw her dirty, knotted, blonde hair frame her scraped, swollen cheeks, from which her moist lips formed a curved smile under the sparkle of her sky-blue eyes. The tubes in her nose and arms no more disfigured her spirit than did the bandaged leg which hung in the air. The room was filled with the spirit of a calm evening sun as the sunset adorned her bedside window. Yet even then I knew this sunset represented the sunrise to come in the months ahead.

Carol greeted me in her normal cheery way, yet in a tone of mature strength. She was not the same child I knew her as when I had said goodbye to her at the beginning of the summer. She didn't have a look of inferiority or fear, but rather a quiet, domineering acceptance of anything asked of her. She began to tell me how excited she was to be picked by God for a special ministry. She winced in pain occasionally while she discussed her future goals to play softball and ride horses again. She slowly showed me that the underlying strength of Jesus Christ gives the ability to look at the good in every situation. It was in this gentle spirit that I saw the healing of a broken body begin to take place.

I sat up with Carol all night as she drifted in and out of sleep filled with terrible dreams of scraping metal and bloody ditches. With each awakening though she held my hand and gave a brave smile. She screamed in agony as she experienced phantom pains of a foot she no longer had. Her entire body hurt, but her spirit soared.

My parents arrived early the next morning before the sun had risen to fill the room. We watched the sunrise together as the nurses checked and double-checked the IV's feeding her tired body. My father, always a strong, yet sensitive man, now lived that which he always preached. He cried occasionally to express the gratitude of still having Carol alive. My mother radiated a song of praise to God for the life of her child. We looked at what Carol had, not what she had lost.

Arrangements were made for Carol to fly to Orange County, California to an advanced medical center only minutes from home. Here she could receive expert care from specialists. Monday evening two days after arriving at my sister's bedside, I rode with her in the ambulance from the hospital to the airport. She was fully conscious, fully happy, and fully beautiful. The bond between us had grown in two days into a tight, interwoven display of emotions. Hurts had been shared with tears, joys had been epressed with songs. Love had grown.

I watched my parents board an air-ambulance Lear jet, along with Carol, neatly packaged in a splint and transportable IV's. The nurse at her side carefully watched her pulse rate as good-byes from relatives were said. I stayed behind the cousins, uncles, and aunts until the moment came when the pilot was closing the door.

I looked into the small, sleek jet at someone I admired and loved for the *courage* she claimed. I fought back the welling of tears which I knew would only depress her. I said good-bye. I watched the plane take off. I knew everything was all right.

I returned to Wheaton to fly to Israel the next day with my class. Now here I was, in the Holy Land, where two-thousand years before Jesus walked and talked and healed. I still didn't hear what the guide was saying about the countryside and history. I was hearing something else. I saw and heard the footsteps of Jesus as He went to the paralytic. I saw the divine hands of the Healer take the broken body of an accepting heart and transform it into a strong active life. I saw Him heal the little children and make the blind men see. I saw him take the remaining leg of my sister, Carol, and make it strong and useful. I saw him take the hearts of my family and create individuals who know what joy through sorrow really is. And I saw Him turn my attitude of despair into an acclamation of joy.

19

Be Happy!
You're Loved!

BOB'S WRITING

How does one measure the healing that happens when love abundant surrounds the patient? Carol was not only surrounded with love, she was inundated with love; first of all from her family.

At one of our pre-dawn breakfasts I remarked to Arvella, "How fortunate Carol is that she is not from a broken home. We will never know what positive healing is taking place as the result of her secure family relationship."

If she would have had her way Carol would have had both Arvella and I with her constantly during her first days and weeks of pain. Surely the love that flowed from mother and dad to child, then sister to sister and brother to sister, had a profound, positive effect in her healing process.

Be happy—you're loved.

Then there were her friends. There is something so special about junior high kids. What a boost they were to her. Arvella and I know that her junior high friends really made a difference in Carol's attitude and outlook. We were deeply impressed. *Carol was happy—she was loved.*

Then there was the love that the hospital staff all sent Carol's way by little deeds—an extra back rub, fluffing up her pillow, playing backgammon during quiet hours, or watching a favorite TV show with her.

Introducing Carol to other children who were patients at the hospital also boosted Carol's spirits. There were the tiny babies with shaved heads with IV's taped to them, little guys who could do a super race with their wheel chairs in the hallways. The nurses also introduced Carol to other girls of her age. One evening Karen was introduced to Carol and it took very little effort for them to become engaged in a lively conversation. Karen empathized with Carol. "I could never do what you have to do—never have your foot again—doesn't it hurt?" But Carol thought Karen was much less fortunate. When she heard Karen tell how she was a diabetic and had to give herself a shot every morning, Carol was not ready to change places with Karen.

Then there were the two lovely young girls who took the time to show Carol their prostheses. They let Carol feel the "Barbie-doll" leg. They showed her how it fit and they answered question after question after question.

There was the resident doctor, who on his free hours would take his guitar and sing for the children. He took time to show Carol a few new chords on the guitar and together they spent many happy moments singing.

The nurses, the physical therapists, the recreational therapists who spent long hours diverting Carol from her pain and discomfort, even the x-ray technicians showed and gave such love.

"Be happy, Carol—you're loved!"

And there was Big Eddie, a wonderful friend of the family. One of our favorite treats as a family was to go to Eddie's Italian restaurant and eat spaghetti made from his own recipe. Eddie came to visit Carol often. When he found out she wasn't eating, he made special dishes for her. Once when he came to visit, the bandages were scheduled for changing, and Carol asked Eddie to stay and hold her hand. Carol's naisl dug into Eddie's hand as she gripped his big hand and held on. Eddie's eyes grew big as he saw the open wounds and experienced Carol's pain. But he never flinched. His love and support boosted Carol's spirits again and again.

Be happy, Carol—you're loved by Eddie!

The gifts, the get well cards and letters began to pour into Carol's room. Hundreds of cards! There were so many it took weeks for Carol to open all of them. But that was the fun part of the day, and she wanted to open them all herself. On the days when she hurt too much, we would open some and read them to her. But they meant the most to her when she could have the fun of opening the envelope and seeing and reading the card herself.

There were the telegrams that really caught her attention and there were two very special ones that she was really excited about. She had lots of fun impressing the doctors and nurses.

The first one read as follows:

THE WHITE HOUSE, WASHINGTON
July 19, 1978

MRS. CARTER AND I WERE DEEPLY DIS-TRESSED TO LEARN OF YOUR SAD ACCIDENT. WE ARE HEARTENED, HOWEVER, BY THE RE-PORTS WE HAVE HAD OF YOUR GREAT COU-

RAGE AND FAITH IN THE FACE OF SUCH ADVERSITY. WE KNOW YOU ARE SUSTAINED BY YOUR FAITH AND BY THE LOVE AND SUPPORT OF YOUR FAMILY. WE SEND YOU OUR WARMEST REGARDS AND OUR PRAYERS FOR A COMPLETE AND RAPID RECOVERY.
WE KNOW YOU WILL HAVE A BRIGHT AND PRODUCTIVE FUTURE AHEAD.

JIMMY CARTER

The second telegram that she read and re-read was this one:

UNITED STATES SENATE
Washington, D.C. 20510
July 14, 1978

Miss Carol Schuller
Children's Hospital of Orange County
1109 West La Veta
Orange, California 92668

Dear Carol:

I am so very sorry to learn about your accident, and I just wanted to write and let you know that you are in my thoughts and prayers.

Perhaps you'll take some encouragement when you learn how well my son Teddy is doing. Following his own operation, Teddy refused to let anything get him down. Just as soon as medically possible, he was up and around and back in school with his friends. He continues to enjoy skiing, loves to race his go-cart, and is a dynamo on a skateboard! In short, Teddy is leading a normal, active and happy life. He once told me that if we have life itself, and the love of family and friends, then we are indeed blessed.

I am sure you will demonstrate your own kind of special courage and determination during these difficult times, Carol, and again, please know that Teddy and I are thinking about you.

With my very best wishes.

Sincerely,

Edward M. Kennedy

There were such beautiful letters from all kinds of churches, from all parts of the nation. The outpouring of faith, hope and love was a tremendous experience for the entire family. We were so impressed when a beautiful brochure came from a neighboring Jewish Synagogue stating that a tree had been planted in Carol's name in the United Synagogue Forest in Israel. It was signed:

To Carol:
  For a speedy recovery
From:
  Temple Beth Emet

"Be happy, you're loved!" was the message that came also via the telephone. Billy Graham called from his home in North Carolina; Steve Garvey and Tommy Lasorda, while they were in Missouri. Both Glenn Ford and John Wayne called more than once. They also sent autographed pictures which Carol instructed me to tape on the wall next to her picture of Jesus. Scrawled in large letters across the photo of John Wayne were the beautiful words he had written: *"Be happy! You're loved!"*

It is true. Love is the highest, happiest feeling in the world. No matter how dark the water, how black the night, how searing the fire, how deep the grief, we can be happy in our sad times if we know we are loved.

The deepest love is the love we experience in a loss, or in a time of grief or sadness. So we are experiencing now one of life's glorious contradictions.

GLADNESS IN SADNESS

And we found this gladness in our sadness because we were surrounded with the love of God through the beautiful people that ministered to us, each in special ways.

One morning, early, the phone at our bedside rang and it was Carol. "Dad, could you bring the binoculars? There is a bird's nest right ouside my window and there are some baby sparrows. I can just see their beaks wide open and the mother bird is feeding them. I don't even have to lift my head from the pillow to see them! You know what, Dad! Everyone has been sending me cards and gifts, and this must be God's gift to me. Isn't that neat?"

Carol was happy! She was loved!

I Can't Wait
Until Tomorrow!

ARVELLA WRITING

Carol's optimistic outlook toward the future and her gallant and positive spirit made it easier for her to face her new problems. It became an inspiration to the family and those around her who had to serve her in her time of need.

Her goals, so small and puny to the average person, were real mountains for Carol to conquer. A few days after the injury, her biggest accomplishment was to grab the bar over her head and lift her body four inches from the bed. Many days later she showed us proudly how she could lift herself a foot up from her bed and shift her entire body so she could be a little more comfortable.

An early goal was to see how long she could last without a pain reliever. There were times when she waited too long, and it was difficult for her to regain control. But there seemed to be a built-in determination that she was going to fight with all she had to become again the active girl she was before the accident.

Then there was the happy clown breathing machine. Two times a day the therapist would come in and give Carol some breathing exercises to prevent pneumonia. She would set a goal as to the number of times Carol needed to do the exercises and the breathing machine not only measured the number but also the intensity. The happy clown face would light up when Carol's breathing goal was reached.

For many weeks there was the challenge of seeing how long the IV would last before she would have to go through the process of watching the nurse search for a vein with her needle. Along with this goal there was also the challenge not to yell or cry while the needle would travel in her arm.

The challenge became a greater one as the weeks went by and there were no more veins. Finally, the climax came late at night when, after her nurse attempted three times to find a vein to receive the IV needle, she sent for help. Four nurses each tried three times and quit. After the twelfth attempt, the decision was made to wait until morning. Carol did some crying that night, but most of the time she was quite a trooper. Early the next morning she joyously awakened us by telephone, announcing that the doctor had ordered, "No more IV's."

Other little goals would often be to see how many glasses of liquid she could drink during the morning and afternoon shift, so that her fever would be kept as low as possible. Her appetite had completely disappeared and she was losing weight rapidly. All kinds of coaxing or threats by the doctor and nurses were forgotten when her tray arrived. Carol responded best to having a goal of four bites at each meal and to reach for that kind of goal.

"I can't wait until tomorrow!" was Carol's comment when she finally learned that she would be coming out of traction. Nine weeks of laying flat on her back was getting terribly boring, uncomfortable and tiresome—all at the same time. What an exciting time for her, but also a fearful time. She had experienced so much pain now that she feared that any new step might be one of pain. This was *not* one of her goals!

When the traction was removed, the real shock of her leg no longer being there hit hard. Carol went into immediate depression and even though we thought we had begun to get used to the loss of her leg, it now was a greater shock, for there were no bars or metal frames giving the optical illusion that somehow it was still there. Now her right leg—slender, long and beautiful—lay stretched out in her bed and next to it was a short, bandaged stump, at least three times larger and ugly against the white sheet—and then there was nothing.

Carol's depression was brief, because now she could move into other positions on her bed, and it meant she could get out of bed.

"I can't wait until tomorrow!" A statement that was so full of anticipation of something great, but also a feeling of being scared. Carol had never faced anything like this before.

"Will I be able to stand on crutches? How will I learn to walk? What if I fall?" *Eager to try but scared to death!* "I can't wait until tomorrow!"

Tomorrow meant that Carol would be helped into a wheelchair for the first time and go down to therapy for the first time.

The physical therapist explained in great detail how they would use a tilt board because Carol would be too weak and dizzy to be put into a standing position. Then the therapist explained all the different exercises that would help Carol to reach her goals. There would be exercises to strengthen her arms to handle crutches, other exercises to make her good leg very strong. The hip and knee of her injured leg would need many different exercises. Carol was eager to go—eager to learn.

Then there were the countless number of questions about her prosthesis. What would it really look like? Can I get it wet? How will I go swimming? What will I do at the beach? Will I have a limp?

"I can't wait until tomorrow!"

Carol's goals and determination label her as her father's daughter. With the same enthusiasm and drive that her daddy daily experiences, Carol is excited about tomorrow. Yes, there are already goals she did not reach, but her healing is much improved because of her goals.

As we finish our journal of *Pearls from Tears,* Carol is home, but her story has only begun. She is confident that God has a special minstry for her to do She is expecting to get her prosthesis for Christmas and is working hard to prepare her body to receive it, and she is planning to walk down the aisle at her sister's wedding—without crutches and without a limp.

Carol found out a few days ago that the infection has returned and she faces her fifth surgery with four more weeks in the hospital. She'll be in isolation, with antibiotics flowing from the IV's through her entire system. When she heard the report, there were no tears, just silence. Finally I broke the silence and said softy, "Carol, God has not failed us yet!" Her answer was swift, "And He won't fail us now either!" Then she added, "Oh, well, at least I'll know all the nurses and everyone at the hospital." With that remark her positive spirit soared again.

Often Carol's closing remark after we have bedtime prayers is "I can't wait until tomorrow!" That's living!

PRESCRIPTIONS FOR PEARLS OF FAITH

Each faith prescription was written on a tiny colored piece of paper and then rolled up and tucked into a clear capsule. Then it was put into a round plastic container with a lable which read: ''Take as needed. Start with one early in the morning.''

What a help these spiritual pills were to Carol morning after morning, and sometimes at night also. She enjoyed choosing a different color, then carefully unrolling the prescription and finding the reference in her Bible. Carol's Bible soon was filled with a rainbow of markers as she left her prescription in the proper place so she could read and re-read them as she wished.

It is a joy to share these spirit-liftern for nearly two months of mornings . . .

o ℞ o

I BELIEVE IN A BIG GOD.

''God is so great that we cannot begin to know Him. No one can begin to understand eternity.''
(Job 36:26)

o ℞ o

THE DIFFICULT I DO IMMEDIATELY, THE IMPOSSIBLE TAKES A LITTLE LONGER.

''. . . With God, everything is possible.''
(Matthew 19:26)

o ℞ o

''LORD, HELP ME TO FIND THE ABUNDANT WAY''

''Jesus told him, 'I am the Way—yes, and the Truth and the Life.''' *(John 14:6)*

o ℞ o

I WILL CLIMB HIGH, CLIMB FAR, MY GOAL THE SKY, MY AIM THE STAR!

''The Lord God is my strength, and He will give me the speed of a deer and bring me safely over the mountains. *(Habakkuk 3:19)*

THANK YOU LORD:
YOU ARE THE LIGHT THAT NEVER GOES OUT,
YOU ARE THE EYE THAT NEVER CLOSES,
YOU ARE THE EAR THAT NEVER SHUTS,
YOU ARE THE MIND THAT NEVER GIVES UP,
YOU ARE THE HAND THAT NEVER STOPS REACHING!

"I can never be lost to Your Spirit! I can never get away from my God! If I go up to heaven, you are there; if I go down to the place of the dead, you are there."

(*Psalm 139: 7, 8*)

○ ℞ ○

WHENEVER I AM TROUBLED AND EVERYTHING GOES WRONG, IT IS JUST GOD WORKING IN ME TO MAKE MY SPIRIT STRONG!

"Dear one, is your life full of difficulties and temptations? Then be happy, for when the way is rough, your patience has a chance to grow. So let it grow, and don't try to squirm out of your problems. For when your patience is finally in full bloom, then you will be ready for anything, strong in character, full and complete." (*James 1:2-4*)

○ ℞ ○

FATHER, I TURN THESE MINUTES OVER TO YOU. DO SOMETHING BEAUTIFUL IN MY MIND, IN MY HEART, IN MY LIFE TODAY!

"For God is at work within you, helping you want to obey him, and then helping you do what he wants." (*Philippians 2:13*)

NOTHING IS EVER TOO HARD TO DO
IF MY FAITH IS STRONG AND MY PURPOSE
  TRUE.
SO, I WILL NEVER GIVE UP AND NEVER STOP
BUT KEEP ON CLIMBING TO MY
  MOUNTAINTOP!

"Tomorrow, I will stand at the top of the hill, with the rod of God in my hand. (Exodus 17:9)

○ ℞ ○

ALL THINGS ARE POSSIBLE TO THOSE WHO
BELIEVE! THE QUESTION IS NOT ONE OF GOD'S
POWER, BUT THE MEASURE OF OUR FAITH IN
GOD'S POWER.

"Jesus said, 'If you had faith even as small as a tiny mustard seed you could say to this mountain, "Move!" and it would go far away. Nothing would be impossible.'" (Matthew 17:20)

○ ℞ ○

I AM BEAUTIFUL! THE TRUE AND LASTING
BEAUTY IS INSIDE. MY BODY IS ONLY TEM-
PORAL. BUT MY SPIRIT IS ETERNAL!

"May your roots go down deep into the soil of God's marvelous love; and may you be able to feel and understand, as all God's children should, how long, how wide, how deep and how high his love really is . . . ." (Esphesians 3:17-19)

○ ℞ ○

I WILL NOT PRAY FOR AN EASY LIFE. I WILL
PRAY TO BE A STRONG PERSON.

". . . The people who know their God shall be strong and do great things." (Daniel 11:32)

WITH EACH DAY I AM MORE CERTAIN EVERYTHING WILL TURN OUT FINE. I HAVE CONFIDENCE THE WORLD CAN ALL BE MINE. THEY'LL HAVE TO AGREE, I HAVE CONFIDENCE IN ME! (Sound of Music)

"In my distress I prayed to the Lord and He answered me and rescued me. He is for me! How can I be afraid? . . . He will help me."

(Psalm 118: 5-7)

○ ℞ ○

HOW MANY APPLES CAN I COUNT IN THE SEED OF MY "ACCIDENT"? GOD ALLOWED IT TO HAPPEN FOR A REASON. HOW MANY GOOD THINGS CAN I THINK OF FOR IT HAPPENING?

"How precious it is, Lord, to realize that You are thinking about me constantly! I can't even count how many times a day your thoughts turn towards me. And when I waken in the morning, you are still thinking of me!" *(Psalm 139: 17-18)*

○ ℞ ○

EVERY WISH IS LIKE A PRAYER WITH GOD. SO, I'LL WISH UPON A STAR, JESUS' STAR, AND THEN I'LL BE A STAR REFLECTING HIS LOVE AND STRENGTH TO ALL AROUND ME.

"Happy are those who long to be just and good, for they shall be completely satisfied."

(Matthew 5:6)

○ ℞ ○

I WILL LET GOD DO THE WORRYING FOR ME, BECAUSE GOD STAYS UP ALL NIGHT ANYWAY.

"Let Him have all your worries and cares, for He is always thinking about you and watching everything that concerns you." *(I Peter 5:7)*

WHEN FACED WITH A MOUNTAIN,
I WILL NOT QUIT.

I WILL KEEP ON STRIVING UNTIL I CLIMB OVER, FIND A PASS THROUGH, TUNNEL UNDERNEATH, OR SIMPLY STAY AND TURN THE MOUNTAIN INTO A GOLDMINE, WITH GOD'S HELP.

"Put these possibilities to work; throw yourself into your tasks so that everyone may notice your improvement and progress. Keep a close watch on all you do and think. Stay true to what is right and God will bless you and use you to help others."

(I Timothy 4:15-16)

○ ℞ ○

I HAVE A POWERFUL, POSITIVE SUSPICION THAT YOU HAVE A PLAN FOR MY TODAY AND MY TOMORROW, AND THAT THIS BEAUTIFUL PLAN IS UNFOLDING EXACTLY AS IT SHOULD.

"I have created you and cared for you since you were born. I will be your God through all your lifetime, yes, even when your hair is white with age. I made you and I will care for you. I will carry you along and be your Savior."   (Isaiah 46:3, 4)

○ ℞ ○

I HAVE COME TO YOU LORD, FOR A NEW LIFT, A NEW LOAD, A NEW LOVE, A NEW LIGHT ON MY LIFE'S ROAD.

"Be strong and of good courage, do not fear or be in dread of them: for it is the Lord your God who goes with you; he will not fail you or forsake you."

(Deuteronomy 31:6 RSV)

IT'S WHEN THINGS SEEM WORST
THAT I DARE NOT QUIT!

(Read Mark 10:46-52)

"Be strong. Be courageous. Do not be afraid . . . for the Lord Your God will be with You . . . He will neither fail nor forsake you."

(Deuteronomy 31:6)

∘ ℞ ∘

I WILL GREET THIS NEW DAY WITH A SONG!

"Listen, O heavens and earth! Listen to what I say! My words shall fall upon you like the gentle rain and dew, like rain upon the tender grass, like showers on the hillside. I will proclaim the greatness of the Lord. How glorious he is! He is the Rock. His work is perfect. Everything he does is just and fair."

(Deuteronomy 32:1-4)

∘ ℞ ∘

LORD, I KNOW THAT TROUBLE IS NOT ALWAYS BAD. IT IS OFTEN YOUR WISE WAY OF PROTECTING ME FROM AN UNKNOWN HAZARD ON THE ROAD: SHELTERING ME FROM A SIN WHICH, UNKOWN TO ME, LURKS IN MY PATH WAITING TO TRICK ME. SO, THANK YOU, LORD!

"I will instruct you and guide you along the best pathway for your life. I will advise you and watch your progress." (Psalm 32:8)

∘ ℞ ∘

I WILL PRAY MY SITUATION UP! THEN GOD CAN BEGIN TO SHOW ME HOW HE CAN TAKE A TRAGEDY AND TURN IT INTO A TRIUMPH!

"All things work together for good to those that love God and keep His commandments."

(Romans 8:28 NASB)

CHRIST'S LIMITLESS RESOURCES
MEET MY ENDLESS NEEDS.

"And the Lord will guide you continually, and satisfy you with all good things, and keep you healthy too; and you will be like a well-watered garden, like an over-flowing spring."

(Isaiah 58:11)

∘ ℞ ∘

GODS LOVE GIVES LIFE DIRECTION!

"For I know the plans I have for you, says the Lord. They are plans for good and not for evil, to give you a future and a hope."   *(Jeremiah 29:11)*

∘ ℞ ∘

WHAT MORE CAN I ASK OF THE SAVIOR
THAN TO KNOW I AM NEVER ALONE—
THAT HIS MERCY AND LOVE ARE UNFAILING
AND HE MAKES ALL MY PROBLEMS HIS OWN.

"I, the Lord your God, hold your right hand; it is I who say to you 'Fear not, I will help you.'"

(Isaiah 41:13a)

∘ ℞ ∘

I HAVE *HOPE!* I will:

   H old

   O n and

   P ray

   E xpectantly

"It is a time to celebrate with a hearty meal, and to send presents to those in need, for the joy of the Lord is your strength. You must not be dejected and sad!"   *(Nehemiah 8:10)*

MAYBE I CAN'T, BUT . . . GOD CAN! IS THERE
SOMETHING TODAY I NEED GOD'S HELP WITH.
I'LL SIMPLY ASK HIM—HE'S THERE!

*"My health fails; my spirits droop, yet God
remains! He is the strength of my heart; he is mine
forever!"*   *(Psalm 73:26)*

○ ℞ ○

WE ALWAYS FIND THAT THOSE WHO WALKED
CLOSEST WITH OUR LORD WERE THOSE WHO
HAD TO BEAR THE GREATEST TRIALS.

                               (ST. THERESA)

*"If your faith remains strong after being tried in the
test tube of fiery trials, it will bring you much praise
and glory and honor . . . ."*   *(I Peter 1:7)*

○ ℞ ○

I WILL STOP WISHING FOR THINGS I COMPLAIN
I DO NOT HAVE, AND START MAKING THE
BEST OF ALL THAT I HAVE GOT!

   WHAT ONE THING AM I MOST THANKFUL
FOR TODAY?

*"In everything you do, stay away from complain-
ing and arguing . . . You are to live clean, innocent
lives as children of God in a dark world . . . Shine
out among them like beacon lights."*

                         (Philippians 2:14, 15)

○ ℞ ○

ATTITUDES ARE MORE IMPORTANT THAN
FACTS. NO MATTER WHAT THE FACTS ARE,
THEY ARE NOT NEARLY AS IMPORTANT AS MY
ATTITUDE ABOUT THEM!

*"Be a new and different person with a fresh
newness in all you do and think."*   *(Romans 12:2)*

IT IS MY RESPONSIBILITY TO SET MY GOALS BIG ENOUGH FOR GOD TO FIT IN THEM. IT IS GOD'S RESPONSIBILITY TO BRING ABOUT THE PEOPLE WHO WILL HELP ME REACH THOSE GOALS.

"We are praying too, that you will be filled with His mighty glorious strength so that you can keep on giving no matter what happens . . . ."

(Colossians 1:11)

○ ℞ ○

TO JESUS . . . EVERY PROBLEM IS AN OPPORTUNITY:

SICKNESS —OPPORTUNITY FOR HEALING
SIN —OPPORTUNITY FOR FORGIVENESS
SORROW —OPPORTUNITY FOR COMPASSION

"For God loved the world so much that He gave his only Son, so that anyone who believes in him shall not perish but have eternal life. God did not send his Son into the world to condemn it, but to save it."

(John 3:16-17)

○ ℞ ○

BEING A CHRISTIAN IS OFFERING MY WHOLE LIFE TO JESUS:

MY MIND —FOR HIM TO THINK THROUGH
MY HEART—FOR HIM TO LOVE THROUGH
MY LIPS —FOR HIM TO SPEAK THROUGH
MY HANDS—FOR HIM TO TOUCH THROUGH.

"Stay close to anything that makes you want to do right. Have faith and love, and enjoy the companionship of those who love the Lord and have pure hearts."

(II Timothy 2:22)

I SHOULD ASK MY HEAVENLY FATHER FOR ANYTHING I WANT, BUT WANT ONLY WHAT MY HEAVENLY FATHER WANTS.

"And in the same way—by our faith—the Holy Spirit helps us with our daily problems and in our praying. For we don't even know what we should pray for, nor how to pray as we should; but the Holy Spirit prays for us with such feeling that it cannot be expressed in words. And the Father who knows all hearts knows, of course, what the Spirit is saying and he pleads for us in harmony with God's own will. And we know that all that happens to us is working for our good if we love God and are fitting into his plans."

(Romans 8:26-28)

○ ℞ ○

NOBODY ELSE CAN DO THE JOB THAT GOD HAS PLANNED FOR ME.
I'VE BEEN CHOSEN ESPECIALLY BY GOD.

"You didn't choose me! I chose you! I appointed you to go and produce lovely fruit always, so that no matter what you ask for from the Father, using my name, he will give it to you."   (John 15:16)

○ ℞ ○

I BELIEVE! I BELIEVE! I BELIEVE!
I'M GOING TO WALK AGAIN!

"He gives power to the faint, and to him who has no might he increases strength. They who wait for the Lord shall renew their strength, they shall mount up with wings like eagles, they shall run and not be weary, they shall walk and not faint."

(Isaiah 40:29-31 RSV)

GOD IS BEHIND ME. HE WILL HELP ME. IF I MUST GO THROUGH DIFFICULT TIMES HE WILL RESCUE ME. I FEEL HIS SPIRIT OF CONFIDENCE SURGING IN MY HEART NOW.

"Dear Friends, don't be bewildered or surprised when you go through the trials . . . Instead, be really glad—because these trials will make you partners with Christ in His suffering, and afterwards you will have the wonderful joy of sharing his glory in that coming day when it will be displayed. So if you are suffering according to God's will, keep on doing what is right and trust yourself to the God who made you, for he will never fail you."

(I Peter 4:12, 13, 19)

○ ℞ ○

THERE HAVE BEEN TIMES, O LORD, WHEN ONLY THROUGH GREAT DIFFICULTY HAVE I LEARNED THE VALUABLE LESSONS. I WAS TOO BLIND TO SEE; TOO ARROGANT TO BELIEVE, OR TOO STUBBORN TO ACCEPT ANY OTHER WAY THAN BY A BED OF PAIN. SO THANK YOU, LORD, FOR LIFE'S PRICELESS TIMES OF FRUITFUL DIFFICULTY.

"The Lord is my shepherd, I shall not want. He makes me lie down in green pastures."

(Psalm 23: 1, 2 RSV)

○ ℞ ○

PEOPLE WHO DEAL IN SUNSHINE, ARE THE ONES WHO DRAW THE CROWDS, THEY ALWAYS DO MORE BUSINESS THAN THOSE WHO PEDDLE CLOUDS.

"For God is our Light and our Protector. He gives us grace and glory. No good thing will be withheld from those who walk along His paths." *(Psalm 84:11)*

WHAT'S MY GOAL FOR TODAY? NOT TO-MORROW, OR THE NEXT DAY, BUT TODAY? MAYBE SHARING SOME CHEER WITH THE NURSES?

"A cheerful heart is a good medicine, but a downcast spirit dries up the bones."

(Proverbs 17:22 RSV)

○ ℞ ○

ALL MY FEARS AND PROBLEMS AREN'T SO BAD— WHEN GOD, THE FATHER IS MY DAD.

"I will be a Father to you, and you will be my sons and daughters." *(II Corinthians 6:18)*

"His unchanging plan has always been to adopt us into his own family by sending Jesus Christ to die for us." *(Ephesians 1:5)*

○ ℞ ○

I HAVE A STRONG, SERENE FEELING THAT GOD IS PLANNING SOMETHING GOOD FOR ME TODAY. I HAVE DEEP FEELINGS THAT SOME-THING WONDERFUL IS IN STORE FOR ME.

"And I am sure that God who began the good work within you will keep right on helping you grow in his grace until his task within you is finally finished on that day when Jesus Christ returns."

(Philippians 1:6)

○ ℞ ○

AS I OBEY GOD'S DIRECTIONS I WILL DISCOVER A COMFORT THAT DOESNT COME FROM A CHANGE IN MY OUTWARD CIRCUMSTANCES. SOMETHING HAPPENS INSIDE ME WHEN I START TO LOVE GOD MORE!

"I will instruct you and guide you along the best pathway for your life; I will advise you and watch your progress." *(Psalm 32:8)*

SAID THE ROBIN TO THE SPARROW, "I SHOULD REALLY LIKE TO KNOW WHY THESE ANXIOUS HUMAN BEINGS RUSH ABOUT AND WORRY SO."

SAID THE SPARROW TO THE ROBIN, "FRIEND, I THINK THAT IT MUST BE THAT THEY HAVE NO HEAVENLY FATHER, SUCH AS CARES FOR YOU AND ME."

"What is the price of five sparrows? A couple of pennies? Not much more than that. Yet God does not forget a single one of them. And he knows the number of hairs on your head! Never fear, you are far more valuable to him than a whole flock of sparrows. (Luke 12: 6-7)

○ ℞ ○

THERE IS NO GAIN WITHOUT PAIN. I MUST BE MAKING HEADWAY BECAUSE I HURT. HALLELUJAH!!

"Whom have I in heaven but you? And I desire no one on earth as much as you! My health fails; my spirits droop, yet God remains! He is the strength of my heart, he is mine forever!" (Psalm 73: 25, 26)

○ ℞ ○

THE STRONGEST TREES ARE FOUND, NOT IN THE SHELTERED NOOKS, BUT IN THE MOST EXPOSED PLACES, WHERE SWEEPS THE FURY OF THE STORM.

"Let me say first of all that wherever I go I hear you being talked about! For your faith in God is becoming known around the world. How I thank God through Jesus Christ for this good report, and for each one of you. God knows how often I pray for you. Day and night I bring you and your needs in prayer to the one I serve with all my might, telling others the Good News about his Son." (Romans 1:8, 9)

LIKE A FRESH BURST OF GOLDEN SUNSHINE
THAT DISSOLVED THE GLOOMY FOG AND
MAKES THE GRASS SPARKLE WITH A GREEN
SHEEN, SO, LORD, YOU HAVE COME INTO
MY MIND AT THE OPENING OF A NEW DAY
ASSURING ME THAT LIFE IS BEAUTIFUL.

"Praise Him from sunrise to sunset." (Psalm 113:3)

○ ℞ ○

LOVE WILL ROLL THE CLOUDS AWAY, TURN
THE DARKNESS INTO DAY!

*"I am persuaded that neither death, nor life, nor
angels, nor principalities, nor powers, nor things
present, nor things to come, nor height, nor depth,
nor any creature, shall be able to separate me from
the love of God, which is in Christ Jesus our Lord."*

(Romans 8:38, 39 KJV)

○ ℞ ○

AT THE BEGINNING OF A NEW DAY, LORD, I SIT
IN A CHOICE SEAT. I WAIT EXPECTANTLY FOR
THE CURTAIN TO GO UP AND FOR THE DRAMA
TO BEGIN.

*"Be glad for all God is planning for you. Be
patient in trouble, and prayerful always."*

(Romans 12:12)

○ ℞ ○

DEAR GOD—INCH BY INCH
ANYTHING'S A CINCH
GIVE ME MORE PATIENCE. AMEN.

*"We can rejoice when we run into problems and
trials for we know that they are good for us—they
help us to learn to be patient. And patience develops
strength of character in us and helps us trust God
more each time we use it until finally our hope and
faith are strong and steady."* (Romans 5: 3, 4)

-111-

GOD WHISPERS TO ME IN MY SADNESS—AND
SHOUTS TO ME IN MY PAIN.

*"God has ascended with a mighty shout, with
trumpets blaring. Sing out your praises to our God,
our King. Yes, sing your highest praises to our King,
the King of all the earth. Sing thoughtful praises."*

(*Psalm 47: 5-7*)

o ℞ o

WHENEVER GOD TAKES SOMETHING AWAY,
HE ALWAYS REPLACES IT WITH
MORE OF HIMSELF.

*"Give your burdens to the Lord. He will carry
them. He will not permit the godly to slip or fall."*

(*Psalm 55:22*)

o ℞ o

I WILL BLOOM WHERE I AM PLANTED!

*"He has given me a new song to sing, of praises to
our God. Now many will hear of the glorious things
he did for me, and stand in awe before the Lord, and
put their trust in him."* (*Psalm 40:3*)

o ℞ o

LORD, SHOW ME THE PERSON YOU WANT TO
SPEAK TO THROUGH MY LIFE TODAY.

*"And so I am giving a new commandment to you
now—love each other just as much as I love you.
Your strong love for each other will prove to the
world that you are my disciples."* (*John 13:34, 35*)

o ℞ o

FEAR KNOCKED ON THE DOOR.
FAITH ANSWERED.
NO ONE WAS THERE!

*"Look! I have been standing at the door and I am
constantly knocking. If anyone hears me calling . . .
and opens the door, I will come in and fellowship
with him and he with me."* (*Revelation 3:20*)